Contents

2nd Edition

GETTING BACK TOGETHER

How to Reconcile with Your Partner—
and Make It Last

Bettie B. Youngs, Ph.D., Ed.D.,
and
Masa Goetz, Ph.D.

Foreword by Suzy Farbman

Adams Media
Avon, Massachusetts

Published by Adams Media, an F+W Publications Company
57 Littlefield Street, Avon, MA 02322 U.S.A.
www.adamsmedia.com

ISBN 10: 1-59337-493-3
ISBN 13: 978-1-59337-493-8
Printed in the United States of America.

J I H G F E D C

Library of Congress Cataloging-in-Publication Data

Youngs, Bettie B.
Getting back together: how to reconcile with your partner—and make it
last / Bettie Youngs and Masa Goetz.—2nd ed.
p. cm.
Includes bibliographical references and index.
ISBN 1-59337-493-3
1. Marriage—Handbooks, manuals, etc. 2. Marital conflict.
3. Reconciliation. I. Goetz, Masa Aiba. II. Title.

HQ734.Y84 2006
646.7'8--dc22

2005026076

This publication is designed to provide accurate and authoritative information
with regard to the subject matter covered. It is sold with the understanding that
the publisher is not engaged in rendering legal, accounting, or other professional
advice. If legal advice or other expert assistance is required, the services of a
competent professional person should be sought.
—From a *Declaration of Principles* jointly adopted by a Committee of the
American Bar Association and a Committee of Publishers and Associations

Many of the designations used by manufacturers and sellers to distinguish their
product are claimed as trademarks. Where those designations appear in this
book and Adams Media was aware of a trademark claim, the designations have
been printed with initial capital letters.

This book is available at quantity discounts for bulk purchases.
For information, please call 1-800-289-0963.

chapter *six*

Are You Ready to Reconcile?

chapter *seven*

Are We Ready to Reconcile?

chapter *eight*

chapter *nine*

chapter *ten*

chapter *eleven*
"A Miracle We're Together":
One Couple's Journey from Separation to Reconciliation 147

chapter *twelve*
Making a Lifetime Commitment:
Advice from Successfully Reunited Couples 161

Foreword

What is happening to you now also happened to me. I, too, was completely devastated by the failure of my marriage and desperate to find answers that would let me put my marriage back together again. Endless questions tormented me: How could this happen? How can I fix it? Is there any hope for us? But I made it through, and you can, too!

Getting Back Together, 2nd Edition distills the knowledge of what is necessary to repair a broken relationship. The practical, step-by-step guidelines in this book show you how to mend the pieces of your relationship, and put the pieces back together into a new relationship that is much better and stronger than before. It is exactly what you need at a time when you feel most vulnerable and are looking for guidance on what to do.

Fear, loneliness, anger, self-recrimination, blame, denial—all these emotions and more plague your mind when your relationship is coming apart at the seams. Although the circumstances seem dire, they are not permanent. If you've recently separated from your partner, don't give up hope for a successful reconciliation! You hold in your hands the possibility of recreating a lasting, fulfilling relationship with your partner. Flying in the face of conventional wisdom—which often advocates "putting it behind you and moving on"—*Getting Back Together, 2nd Edition* clearly shows you what must be done to give yourself the best chance of reconciliation. This book takes you on the journey of what really happens when couples split up and then successfully reconcile.

Would you be surprised to learn that separation can be good for a relationship? *Getting Back Together, 2nd Edition* explains how being apart can actually give you the best chance of getting back together!

From my own experience with infidelity and the long journey back to reconciliation, I especially appreciate the advice on issues such as: the importance of temporarily detaching from the desire to reconcile immediately; the need to discover and strengthen your own inner resources; the need for necessary changes to take place before reconciliation; and the importance of deciding what your core values are and how they will be expressed in the relationship. Advice on how to know when you are ready to reconcile and what to do after you reunite makes this a comprehensive guide that coaches you every step of the way. This book will help you formulate a proactive plan that will not only be the basis for a better relationship, but also the foundation for a stronger and happier you!

Couples who separate and get back together know what it takes to rebuild a relationship. They have succeeded in accomplishing what most regard as impossible: overcoming the seemingly insurmountable problems of the past, and creating deeply loving, lasting, and renewed relationships with their former partner. *Getting Back Together, 2nd Edition* presents numerous true stories that show how real people deal with the many problems that arise during separation. Their experiences make for inspiring and enlightening reading.

This book is a must-read for everyone who has broken up with a partner and is searching for hope and guidance in getting back together. Its soothing advice will provide you with stability and direction for managing the critical and painful time of separation from your loved one. Authors Bettie B. Youngs and Masa Goetz have succeeded in writing a book that is honest, clearheaded, practical, down-to-earth, and helpful for those who are devastated by the loss of their partner and are searching for ways to reconcile. I am enormously pleased that so many people—including you—may be helped!

—Suzy Farbman, author, *Back from Betrayal:*
Saving a Marriage, a Family, a Life

Acknowledgments

So many people have been instrumental in creating the inspiration and material for this book: the clients whose struggles and successes form the basis of this work; the couples who were interviewed and freely shared their experiences of separation and reunion; and the professional colleagues who offered their valuable insight and support. We thank you for being so open and willing to share your journey through separation and reconciliation with us. Certainly you form the heart of this book. A warm thanks to our publisher, Adams Media, and to editor Danielle Chiotti, for their support and belief in this work; to Susan Heim from our staff for her skillful editing work; and to Bill Gladstone at Waterside for helping this project come to fruition—and for his friendship over the years. Also, a most special thanks to family and friends whose love and friendship sustain us.

Bettie B. Youngs, Ph.D., Ed.D., and Masa Goetz, Ph.D.

Dear Reader:

- Are you mourning the loss of a love you thought would last forever?

- Are you unwilling to put everything you cherished behind you and start all over again?

- Has your relationship crumbled under the weight of betrayal, addiction, or broken promises?

- Are you torn between advice to "let go"—and your heart's desire to find a way to be together again?

- Have you and your partner separated and reconciled before—only to find the same issues unresolved?

- Do your beliefs direct you to seek reconciliation rather than walk away from your vows?

- Are you willing to take the steps that might lead you back to a renewed and more loving relationship—but wondering how to begin?

If you answered "yes" to any of the questions above, chances are that you're going through a devastating time right now. The pain of your loss may feel unendurable, and your mind keeps churning with the same thoughts over and over again: "How did this happen?" "Why can't we make things work out?" "I never thought I'd find myself in this position." You know your relationship is in more pieces than Humpty Dumpty, yet you hope it can be put together again.

You may feel as if you are the only one going through this experience right now, but separation is much more common than you may think. Although some couples separate permanently, the numbers show that separation does not have to lead to divorce. Despite divorce statistics that have held steady at approximately 50 percent for all first-time marriages, Americans still value the ideals of marriage with a lifelong partner. What is hidden in these statistics is the number of individuals who do reconcile with and remarry the partners they originally separated from—a figure that some experts have estimated ranges up to 14 percent. In actual numbers, this would mean that of the almost one million divorces reported in the latest U.S. Census Bureau figures, approximately 140,000 divorced couples eventually reconciled. There are many more couples, as high as 80 percent according to some accounts, who informally separate for some period of time during their marriage and then reunite.

These numbers prove that there is hope. Countless women and men have been in your situation, and have found their way back to a loving relationship with their partner. Some decided to enter counseling. Others worked toward solving their problems on their own when they saw that their relationship was in danger of breaking apart. In some cases, there was little change; the couples settled for things remaining much the same as they were. But in others cases, change was dramatic—the relationship was significantly improved.

What do these couples know that you don't? What have they done that you can learn from? The important changes these couples made are an example for others to follow. By listening to their stories—from painful separation to loving reunion—we discovered a practical model of hope for others to follow. This does not mean that all marriages can or should be put back together. When relationships are destructive and there is little hope of change, they may need to end.

So, how do you begin? You've already taken the first step by deciding to become pro-active. In this book, we'll show you how to make separation work for the relationship instead of against it; how to get your self-confidence and energy back; and what steps to take that can lead to a renewed relationship. Separation can be a time of tremendous growth and discovery for you—one that puts you in a much better position to heal your relationship and achieve a successful and long-lasting reconciliation.

If your partner is willing to read this book at the same time—all the better! You'll both be on the path to greater growth and change. But if your partner is not ready yet, then begin on your own, perhaps with the assistance of counseling. Do reach out for support and guidance if you need it.

If you believe that there is a future for yourself and your partner, and you are willing to take the steps to achieve your goal, then this book is for you. You will be shown how to make a separation work for the relationship rather than against it; how to increase your inner strength so that the relationship has a stronger foundation; and how to go through the steps of discovery and renewal to a successful reconciliation. With specific strategies and easy-to-understand principles that you can apply right away, *Getting Back Together, 2nd Edition* helps you make your way back into a loving and enduring relationship.

Sometimes, what looks like the end is really an opportunity for a new beginning. So pay attention to the possibilities ahead of you. Rather than regarding separation as a failure, take one step at a time on this journey of personal growth and keep your focus on reconciliation and a much stronger, more loving, and committed relationship.

—Bettie B. Youngs, Ph.D., Ed.D., and Masa Goetz, Ph.D.

Please note that throughout this book, we have alternated the use of "he" or "she" for ease in reading, although the situations and principles apply equally to both men and women.

chapter *one*

Getting Back Together:
What You Must Know Now

What you thought would last forever seems to be ending. Words of "I love you" have been replaced by silence or accusations and recriminations. Tears and fears abound. You remember the love you shared and the familiar routine that was your day-to-day life. You feel sadness and disappointment over the dreams and expectations you held for your lives and this relationship, thinking they may never be realized. You wonder if things can ever be the way they were when things were good. You wonder if getting back together is possible: Will she ever love me again? Can I ever trust him again?

Right now, you may be feeling that your relationship is so damaged it's hard to see how it can be repaired. Or maybe one of you doesn't even want to try. Maybe she left and is now seeing someone new. Or maybe he says, "I just need some space," but you wonder if he's buying time or just doesn't want to break it to you that he doesn't really intend to work toward reconciling the differences between you. Or he wants to get back together, but you're wondering if you can or should trust his efforts. You wonder if it's really possible to rekindle love despite all that has happened.

A million and one questions; a heavy heart; decisions to make: Can love be repaired and, if so, can you repair yours? Take heart. It is possible to rebuild a broken relationship, and make it stronger and better.

Separation: The First Step to Getting Back Together

Are you separated, or afraid that separation is inevitable? As difficult as it is to believe right now, being apart for a while might actually be the best thing that could happen to your relationship. Time apart gives you a chance to step back and gain insight about what's wrong between you. Removed from the old struggles that caused so much pain, you can now take a time-out to focus on yourself—your needs, goals, and expectations. You have breathing room to regain your emotional balance, and the space to get to know yourself and decide what you want from the relationship. This can be a very constructive period—a time of renewal in which needed changes can be made and problems resolved. Painful though it is, separation can be the first step to getting back together again—truly back together, not just physically under the same roof, but together emotionally and spiritually. It can serve as a time for discarding destructive old patterns of relating and learning new ways that build a solid and healthy relationship. This is an opportunity for both of you to restore yourselves, to grow, and to see how you can come back together more deeply committed than ever.

Chances are, right now you're the only one making an effort to salvage this relationship, and you feel quite alone. That's okay, because there's much to do that you must do by yourself. This book will show you how. It will take you through the steps that can help you do things on your own and strengthen you as a person so that, eventually, a new relationship between you and your partner can take place.

Couples Do Separate and Get Back Together Again

Here's a surprising fact: Approximately 80 percent of all married couples separate for two months or longer sometime during their marriage. And nearly 14 percent of all couples who actually divorce remarry each other. Marriage counselors know that nearly two-thirds of all divorced couples would choose to remain married to each other if only they could resolve the primary difficulties that led to the breakup. Pat and Martin are typical of couples that started out with a series of unproductive separations, but then learned to use separation as a constructive period to resolve their major difficulties during their time apart.

Pat and Martin constantly argued about Martin's drinking and the effect it was having on their relationship. Though Martin was a charming man when sober, his angry tirades when he drank caused Pat to pack her things and move out a number of times. But she always gave in to Martin's promises that "things will be different this time. Just give me a chance to prove it to you." Pat found his protestations persuasive, and she always returned. But Martin returned to his old ways time and time again. After the third separation, Pat knew there would have to be real and lasting changes before she could go back to him. This time, when Pat saw Martin's tears and heard his promises to change his behavior if she would come back, she refused to give in. Even though she didn't want her marriage to end, she knew she couldn't live with him unless he got help for his drinking. She moved out again, vowing not to return this time until he dealt with his alcohol addiction and the two of them worked out their problems.

Realizing Pat was serious about staying away, Martin was forced to face his difficulties and find solutions. He admitted himself into a rehab program and sought help for his alcoholism. Confronting hard issues and working through them helped Martin restore confidence in himself and enabled him to commit to recovery. During this time of separation, Pat also worked on her own healing by getting support and regularly attending meetings for family members of alcoholics. As they both progressed and Martin committed to maintaining his sobriety, Pat allowed herself to become cautiously optimistic about their chances for reconciliation. One year later, they are together again, both dedicated to building on the gains they have made and thriving in a relationship that satisfies both of them.

Separation Is Not the Problem—It's the Symptom

Unfortunately, when couples separate, one or both partners too often focus on the separation as the problem and rush back into the relationship, ignoring the underlying causes that led to the breakup. Unless the focus is directed to the causes, being back together won't change things. Separation is not the cause of the problems you and your partner have; it's the symptom of them, as shown by what happened with Sharon and Matt.

"Matt seemed to have everything I wanted in a man," Sharon said, "except for one drawback: He wouldn't commit to getting married. His first marriage had ended in a really painful divorce, and he didn't want to risk a failed marriage ever again. But we had been together for two and a half years, and we really loved each other. I wanted marriage, so I moved in with Matt, telling myself that because we loved each other so much, it was just a matter of time before he would change his mind about us marrying. But another full year passed, and still he said no to marriage.

"I really resented his resistance to us getting married, so I moved out a couple of times, hoping it would shock him into proposing to me. But as soon as he started saying 'maybe' or 'perhaps' marriage was in our future, I'd go running back to him before the issue was really resolved. But because no ring was ever bought—or date was ever set—I became unhappier.

"Added to this was the pressure I felt from friends and family. I was raised to believe that you fell in love, got married, and had a family. Every time I saw my mother, she would ask when Matt and I were going to get married. Even my girlfriends kept asking when we were going to 'tie the knot.' I'd go home to Matt feeling depressed and doubting if he really loved me. We'd end up having terrible arguments.

"Finally, I told Matt I was moving out for the last time—and that I was not coming back unless there was a not only a commitment to get married, but a ring and a wedding date set.

"Being without Matt again was just awful. It was such a painful time. The good news is that separation was the best thing that could have happened. Our being apart was painful to Matt as well, and this drove us into counseling. With help, we began talking through our fears, needs, and expectations, and we were able to resolve the issues that were tearing us apart. We've learned so much and understand each other so much better now. Being apart worked for us. It gave us a chance to gain perspective and bring everything out in the open, and to find a way to work through the issues that kept us from having the relationship we really wanted. We feel really solid about our relationship now and are planning our wedding for the spring."

Use Separation as a Time to Make Necessary Changes

As Sharon realized, another common mistake of troubled couples is to try to get back together too soon. One or both hope that if they "get together and try harder," things will work out. This is understandable. Loneliness and fear of facing the future alone can lead one or both partners to want to reconcile as soon as possible. But if you concentrate solely on getting back together, the work each of you needs to do to make reconciliation successful doesn't get a chance to happen. For example, you may need individual and couples counseling; treatment for alcohol, drug, or other addictions; or healing of old emotional wounds that negatively affected your relationship. Unresolved issues make for unsuccessful reconciliations. The deeper changes that could occur while you're apart—changes reflecting personal growth that could lead to a more satisfying relationship—

usually don't get a chance to happen. The original problems will still be there and continue to cause difficulties. The cycle may begin again, with another separation and another quick reconciliation—and if the underlying problems are still not addressed, the end result might be permanent separation. That's what happened to Irene and George.

"Nothing hurt as much as when Irene and I separated," George said about their three-year marriage that recently collapsed. "Irene is a wonderfully warm, fun, loving woman—and we have so much in common. Most of the time, we got along really well. But every once in a while, I'd get really insecure and jealous, and start grilling her about one thing or another. Sometimes it was about whom she went to a business lunch with; or if she went on an out-of-town business trip, I'd be convinced she was seeing someone. I knew it wasn't realistic. With my rational mind, I knew she was totally trustworthy. But my mother cheated on my father, and somewhere in the back of my mind I thought it could happen to me, too. The end came when I accused her of having an affair after she had attended a training seminar. She said she couldn't live with my 'continuous and unfounded suspicions' and moved out.

"I begged her to stay, but she said she needed to get away and clear her mind. I started to panic. Irene was everything to me. I told her I was starting counseling (something she'd always asked me to do) and would do whatever else it took to get her back. The first few weeks, we just spoke on the phone and e-mailed each other. I was really careful not to ask her what she was doing so she wouldn't think I was checking up on her. The next month we met for dinner five or six times and went for walks afterward. We had some really good discussions, and it looked like we were working things out. Irene said she missed me, and that gave me a big lift. We were getting along so well that about a month later we got back together. I was convinced that I had a handle on my insecurities and that things would be different. Unfortunately, I got overconfident and stopped going to counseling. My old, suspicious behavior started again, and after warning me several times, Irene left me—this time for good."

This is an example of how focusing on getting back together too soon, rather than on resolving root issues, can cause a permanent separation. George and Irene had the makings of a good relationship: They had many shared interests, enjoyed each other's company, valued the same things, and basically, had a satisfying life. If George had used as much time as he needed during the separation to resolve his issues, he might have succeeded in permanently mending their relationship. If the focus had been on resolving those issues rather than prematurely ending their separation, both could have avoided what predictably happened—the permanent end of their relationship.

Separation as a Time-Out

Accounts of couples who have successfully reunited show that separation can be thought of as a time-out. It gives each partner the time and space to work on the personal problems that led to the breakup. Just as important, separation gives respite to the severed relationship; this is a well-needed break from constantly being tested by stressful situations just when the relationship is at its weakest. Physical distancing allows the old angers and hurts that get in the way of communication to lessen while change is taking place. It gives you the chance to stand back and evaluate the relationship from another perspective, identify its strengths and weaknesses, and discover the ways in which it does and does not work for you. Just as important, it gives you the opportunity to rebuild your confidence so that you can bring a renewed and revitalized sense of yourself—a "new and improved" you—to the relationship. This makes getting back with your partner possible.

Although separation is deeply painful, it is an opportunity to work out your differences and come together in a more deeply committed relationship. The reunited couples who were interviewed for this book say that an important part of the quality of their current relationship is due to the opportunity for self-development that separation provided. While they would have preferred to work out their problems within the marriage, having a time-out gave them an unparalleled impetus for growth and change. In fact, the most common response of couples who were asked, "In looking back, what would you have done differently?" was, "We would have taken a little bit longer before getting back together and used that time to resolve a couple of other issues between us." They also agreed that the level of commitment and caring they have with each other now was made possible largely by their growth during the separation.

Key Ingredients of a Successful Separation and Reconciliation

Separation doesn't have to mean the end of your relationship. Many couples separate and then come back together in mutually satisfying relationships. But reconciliation, like all desirable goals, requires work and commitment. It takes clear thinking to accept the separation as a needed break from seemingly irreconcilable conflict, to understand its causes, and to begin the hard work of resolving the problems that caused it. It takes patience and dedication to create a successful reconciliation. Our goal in this book is to help you use this time of separation constructively, so that you can come back together in a relationship that is deeply satisfying for both of you. In the following chapters, we'll give you specific suggestions on the work that lies ahead. Briefly, here's a preview of the key principles:

- Take care of yourself. When you're hurting or feeling unsure of yourself, it can be easy to neglect your needs. Do those things that keep you physically healthy and psychologically strong.

- Get to know yourself. Find out who you are and what you want at THIS point in your life. Only when you know yourself, and decide that you hold the key to your own happiness, can you be whole and happy with someone else.

Inventory your values and goals, and chart a course for your own well-being from this point forward.

- Work on strengthening your own identity. Seek out those things that bring meaning and purpose to your life, rather than living life through someone else. Create a lifestyle that revolves around your values, needs, and those things that inspire you to live your personal best.

- If you and your partner are still speaking, agree on ground rules that will govern your actions during your time apart. These might include being faithful to one another, agreeing on how time and activities with the children will be handled, and whether you will enter counseling together.

- Think through and create a strategy for recreating a healthy and loving relationship with your partner. Commit to doing those positive actions that are more likely to create a new and lasting relationship.

- Prepare for those times when you seem to be unable to go forward, when your plan seems to have failed or backfired—at least temporarily. Know what compromises you will—and won't—make in terms of modifying that plan.

- Build a support network of people who root for you and your well-being. Take time to be with those who inspire you and can sustain you in good times as well as in uncertain times.

- Communication and trust are the keys to intimacy. Learn the art of how to listen and talk without judgment and with an open heart. Commit to a style of communicating with your partner that leads to being able to share your thoughts and feelings opening and authentically—and that allow your partner to do so as well.

- Commit to resolving old habits and destructive behaviors that damage your relationship, and learn what is needed to make love flourish. There are reasons for feelings of hurt, pain, anger, resentment, or the desire to retaliate. Beneath them is a tender place of truth—a place where you need to be comfortable so that you can allow yourself to be vulnerable in making the changes that are necessary to make love flourish. Find the courage to visit this place of truth for you.

- Think of reconciliation as the start of a new relationship. Being back together is not the end, but a new beginning. Like all relationships, it will have its ups and downs. Be realistic.

- Commit to sustaining your new relationship. Once you're back together, use your newfound skills to strengthen and deepen your friendship and love. Consider the health of your new relationship whenever decisions are made, and make your relationship a high priority in your life.

When you reunite with your partner, you won't find the old relationship that didn't work, but a new one that could work. Of course, it's not always possible to turn a dysfunctional relationship into a good one. But if there's still caring underneath the pain and disappointment, and if you both want to reconstruct a relationship with the person you still love, know that love can be rekindled and that the pieces can be put back together again.

Thousands of people just like yourself have separated and found their way back to a more loving, fulfilling relationship. The love you seek may seem elusive, but you have within you right now the fortitude and the resources you need to give yourself the best chance of success. As you dedicate yourself to your goal, know that you will gain strength and confidence with each step you take. So take a deep breath and go forward!

Questions for Reflection

1. What are my feelings at this moment about our separation and the future of our relationship?

   _____

   _____

2. Am I ready to begin constructing a plan to better myself and my relationship? Do I feel optimistic that my partner and I can use our separation constructively to build a new relationship?

   _____

   _____

3. Where does my partner "stand" on our relationship—is he willing to work on our problems, distancing himself, or wanting instant reconciliation? How are we relating right now?

   _____

   _____

4. What could I do at this time to gain inner strength? What resources do I have—friends, family, books, counseling, career, religion, etc.—that will help me to become a better "me"?

   _____

   _____

5. What positive aspects of myself, my partner, or our relationship could I build on? What things do I see as being "right" about our relationship?

   _____

   _____

chapter *two*

Just Getting Back with Your Partner Isn't Enough: The Dangers of a Premature Reunion

"I know if I could just talk to Julie, we'd be able to work things out. But how can I convince her that she should give us another chance when she won't see me or take my calls?" Tom asked, his voice filled with anxiety and frustration. He had been calling Julie, leaving message after message on her answering machine, but she never called back. As Tom tried to cope with his pain, he was obsessed by one thought: "If only we could get back together, things would work out somehow."

Especially in those first few days and weeks of separation, you may feel as Tom did—that getting back together as soon as possible is the best solution to your problems. You tell yourself, "If he comes back, I'll make sure that things are different." "I'll spend more time with her." "I won't lose my temper or be so demanding." "I'll cut down on my drinking." "I'll do whatever it takes to get him back!" Within these hopes is your desperate want for the pain and hurt to stop; you want your life back to normal again. But determination and resolution—no matter how strong and sincere—are, unfortunately, not enough. It takes more than good intentions to get your partner back, and to ensure that the relationship will be a healthy one.

Negative History and Dysfunctional Patterns of Behavior

Two of the chief saboteurs of a successful reunion are negative history and dysfunctional patterns of behavior. Negative history is the accumulation of all the angry, painful, destructive events that have happened to the two of you as a couple. It's the relationship's emotional baggage—resentments, suspicions, and insecurities—we carry around. Automatic triggers and reactions set off destructive emotional responses and dysfunctional patterns of behavior, creating hurt and pain for you and your partner. When each partner is dealing with the worst behavior of the other, it's hard to convince that person to want you back.

Relationships require careful tending to stay healthy. Destructive ways of interacting and the accumulation of hurts gradually erode and destroy relationships. Painful memories of the hurtful things that have happened between you—such as broken promises, infidelity, heated fights—can be triggered by thoughtless words and actions.

Remember the times you vowed you would handle things differently, but couldn't stop reacting to your partner in the same negative ways? "I know better," you say, "but he pushes my buttons." That's exactly right. When you've lived with someone long enough, you both know all the buttons to push. Even innocent words or actions can trigger the old, destructive emotions and ways of interacting. When he's a few minutes late, you flash back to the time he missed an important event because he never bothered to call. When he lowers his voice on the phone, you recall his old girlfriend who suddenly started calling because she had just gotten a divorce. A look is interpreted as impatient; a tone of voice is heard as signaling anger, sarcasm, or a putdown. These triggers, rooted in painful memories, must be resolved or they destroy any possibility of a resolution. This can be seen most clearly in couples that reunite prematurely and don't allow time for old negative memories to fade and more current, positive experiences to build up.

The Dangers of Rushing into Reconciliation

When someone tells you, "Oh, yes, we tried getting back together, but it just didn't work out," often what happened is that they hurried back together too soon.

Do you want to reunite temporarily or permanently? When you first get back together after a separation, things may seem wonderful, even better than ever. You're in a kind of "honeymoon" stage, with all the excitement, warmth, and passion of a new romance. But eventually, the old problems and old habits of interacting begin to creep back—unless you've made some fundamental changes in the way you think about yourself, your partner, and the relationship.

Couples in troubled relationships who reunite prematurely usually go through a four-stage cycle that leads to a temporary reunion—and, eventually, a permanent ending of the relationship.

The Four-Stage Cycle of Premature Reconciliation

Stage One: Disintegration. The problems of the relationship seem overwhelming. The negative history and dysfunctional behavior accumulate. Anger, resentment, and destructive actions escalate, leading to increasingly bitter arguments and emotional withdrawal. Attempts to deal with the problems are ineffectual. Though there is love and caring beneath the pain and confusion, separation seems the only solution.

Stage Two: Separation. One or both partners distance themselves from the relationship (emotionally and/or physically), deciding the problems are too much to overcome. Both partners wonder what went wrong, wish they could work things out, and believe that if only their partner would change or some compromises were made, all would be well. The real problems and underlying causes are usually unacknowledged or pushed into the background. Little if any attempt is made to understand or resolve them.

Stage Three: Premature Reunion. Separation and loss of a partner is extremely painful. The most common reaction is to promise anything, vow to "try harder," and reach out desperately to try to bring your loved one back as quickly as possible. But the problems are quickly as overwhelming the second time around. If underlying problems haven't been addressed, and effective solutions found, the same destructive patterns of behavior quickly return. The couple comes back together, but little if anything has been resolved. The same cycle of problems that led to the first separation is repeated, usually with greater intensity. Resentments and withdrawal intensify until the only solution seems to be a permanent separation.

Stage Four: Permanent Separation or Divorce. One or both partners are convinced that everything possible has been done to give the relationship a chance to survive, but to no avail. After all, they have already tried reconciliation. They've "tried harder" in the ways they knew how. They've put their best efforts into making a go of it, but things just didn't work out. At this point, one or both people feel they have no choice but to end the relationship.

It doesn't have to be this way. There is a model that can lead to a successful and permanent reconciliation.

Successful Reconciliation

Stage One: Disintegration. The problems of the relationship seem overwhelming. The negative history and dysfunctional behavior accumulate. Anger, resentment, and destructive actions escalate, leading to increasingly bitter arguments or emotional withdrawal. Attempts to deal with the problems are ineffectual. Though there is love and caring beneath the pain and confusion, separation seems the only solution.

Stage Two: Separation. One or both partners distance themselves from the relationship. Separation is seen as a necessary step, a time apart that allows both partners space to grow and an opportunity to create a wholly new relationship. Rather than attempting to solve problems by demanding change from the other partner, the focus is on individual self-discovery and growth. New ways of viewing the relationship, new patterns of behavior, and new ways of meeting each other's needs that can lead to a strong and mutually satisfying relationship are acquired.

Stage Three: Preparation. Because of the new perspective gained in Stage Two, and actively working toward healing unresolved personal issues, each partner starts to perceive the other in more positive ways. Feelings of desperation begin to give way to a new sense of hope. As communication improves and trust is established, both partners begin talking, openly and honestly, about their fundamental feelings and desires. They begin to see each other as desirable once more and start talking seriously about reconciliation.

Stage Four: Successful Reconciliation. Both partners have grown and matured. There is now much more understanding of themselves, their mates, and the relationship. They have created a healthy mutual interdependence. Both have learned more about themselves and what it takes to be in a mutually satisfying relationship—in particular, this relationship. Both partners have a better understanding of how to love and live together in ways that satisfy the needs of both. Out of the ashes of the old relationship, they have created a new and better relationship that works for both of them.

The first step in the cycle of a successful reconciliation is to understand the positive role that a separation can play.

How Healing Starts

As we've been saying, one of the major benefits of the separation stage is the time and space apart. During the early stages of the separation, if you are in communication with each other, it's likely that you're still having the same arguments in the same destructive ways. You need a period of respite to recover from the bitterness and pain, and to begin to let go of the hurt. As you learn new ways to get your needs met, the old patterns will be replaced by new ones that work for the relationship. For example, if you were overly dependent on your partner for companionship but have started to develop new interests and friends, you have something new to bring to the relationship that adds vitality.

> During their separation, Tom realized that he had intimidated Julie by his confrontational communication style—and that it drove her away. He knew he needed to try a different approach. He sent her a card with a simple message saying that he cared for her deeply and he hoped she was well. He didn't hound her with frantic calls, but rather, he called every few days. He made a point of not being inquisitive, but simply told her that he was saying hello, that he was thinking of her, and that she should "call if you need anything."

Tom was learning how to communicate without demanding that he hear only what he wanted to hear. It was the start of a new cycle of positive interactions between them—one that led to their talking, getting into couple's counseling, and, eventually, reconciling. Again, this is one of the many benefits of using separation as a time to work on yourself. As you learn to do this, your frustration about being separated lessens. You begin to achieve perspective on your relationship—and you take one of the first steps toward a successful reconciliation.

Why You Need Time Apart

It's natural to hope that your partner will come back and that things will be the way they "used to be." But that's not all you really want. You want to be together in a relationship that is better than it was. That's why it's important to use your time apart constructively.

When you separate, you're forced to examine fundamental issues about yourself, your partner, and the relationship. At first, these issues can feel so frightening or overwhelming that your first instinct is to run back to the seeming safety of the old relationship's habits. When the pain of separation engulfs you, it's easy to forget the anger, hurt, resentment, and other negative feelings you had. Fear of losing your partner forever, being alone, not finding someone else to love, or not being able to survive financially on your own can lead you to prematurely rush back to the relationship. But if the relationship is to have a chance, you need distance. Separation provides an opportunity to step back and look at things from a more realistic perspective. Take the time you need to begin to identify the underlying problems and work toward solving some of the bigger ones.

You need time to regain your emotional equilibrium and start to heal, time to get to know yourself and discover what you want. If you take the time to get to know yourself and your needs, and to build upon your strengths, you have a much better chance of attracting and drawing your partner back and keeping him or her.

What Really Went Wrong in the Relationship?

In addition to feeling more emotionally stable and being able to once again tend to your day-to-day activities, it's important to be honest about what really went wrong. You need to identify the underlying causes that led to the separation. If you sweep the problems under the rug and decide to ignore them, they will resurface. Too often we see the problems as being the other partner's fault—his bad attitude or her selfish behavior. This is usually what the partner who has been left wants to talk about during the first few weeks of counseling. We remember all the painful events, conflicts, irritating characteristics, and disappointments in the relationship. But these are mostly symptoms of more fundamental problems. Concentrating on fixing the symptoms—rather than on finding and resolving the basic causes—can lead to a downward spiral of frustration, counterproductive behavior, and destructive reactions. Underlying causes of relationship problems are as varied as the couples involved. However, they generally fall into one or more of the following categories. (By the way, we will be helping you learn new skills to surmount each of these challenges throughout this book.)

Unfulfilled Expectations

Everyone enters into a relationship with an idea of what it "should" be like, especially the belief that being in a relationship will magically create happiness and fulfillment. You've probably said or had some of these thoughts yourself: "I want my marriage to be as happy as my best friend's marriage," or "I want to be loved like my father loved my mother." Sometimes one person expects the other person to automatically know what he wants, thinking: "If you loved me, you'd know what I want."

Other expectations center around who takes responsibility for certain things, such as, "I expect him to keep my car in running order because that's what men do," or "I expect her to cook because that's what women do," or "She should take the kids to school and pick them up because she's their mother." The list of expectations is endless and can be based on anything, from childhood experiences in your own family, to the influence of friends, or what we see in the media. These are the experiences that define for us what is "right" or "normal." A good example is opening Christmas presents. Does your family exchange and open them on Christmas Eve or on Christmas morning? Chances are, whatever feels "right" to you is what your family did when you were growing up. Big things, little things: We all have a belief in how they should be done. What's important is how these expectations play out—and exert influence—on the two of you as a couple.

Inability to Communicate

When communication breaks down, so does the relationship, and you're headed for tough times—which makes communication even more difficult. There are so many areas in which communication can break down:

- How each of you interprets what the other says

- Whether you and your partner remain silent and pretend everything's all right when problems come up

- How well you listen to each other

- How much time you make for real communication

- Whether you're able to reveal your true feelings and desires, and then work together to affect a positive outcome

Unfortunately, we often don't express ourselves honestly because of our emotional pain and anger, fear of losing control and lashing out at our partner, or worry that our partner might react negatively. Or we are worried about becoming vulnerable. If others know too much about us, they may use the information against us later on.

The feeling that you are not understood, that you can't really talk to your partner or can't be yourself around him, is a real blow to your heart. Communication is so complex, yet so important, that we have devoted an entire chapter to it (Chapter 8, "Communication: What Works and Why").

Lack of Intimacy

In an intimate relationship, you trust your partner enough to be willing to be vulnerable. Couples who are able to talk about their deepest desires, fears, goals, and expectations and who know they will not be judged negatively say they are "on the same page." They have the safety of knowing their partner will continue to love and accept them throughout the ups and downs of life. Couples who communicate at this level experience their relationship as deeply rich and rewarding. They consider themselves best friends, lovers, and companions—a team that meets the challenges of life together. You are important to your partner because of who you are, not because of your parenting or spousal role, or your career, but because you're you. If you can't trust that your partner is "in your camp" emotionally, intimacy breaks down and the relationship erodes.

Taking Stock of the Situation

Are you separated, or is separation inevitable? If so, it's an ideal time to take stock, not just about the state of your relationship, but about YOU. Now is the time to take care of yourself; it's the first step in moving forward. Following are some questions to help you take a good look at how you're coping with things at this very moment. Be really honest with yourself when you answer each one. These questions are a way to get you thinking about where you are in your life right now. Some of them you will be able to answer easily and quickly. Others you might want to ponder and write about in a journal. Over the next few months, as you grow and heal, your answers may change. These questions are an excellent way for you to gain perspective on your current situation and keep track of your progress in the time period ahead.

Emotional Balance: Are you newly separated and dealing with raw pain that hurts so much you can barely function? Or have you been separated for long enough that the pain is now tolerable and you have recovered some of your emotional equilibrium?

Physical Health: Have your eating and sleeping habits changed as a result of the separation? Have you let yourself become run down? Or have you gone the other way and become fanatical about your diet and exercise (trying to look good and win him back)—to the point of overdoing it?

Children: How are they handling the separation? Have you worked out a custody arrangement with your spouse? Is it working fairly smoothly, or is it causing problems? How has being a single parent affected your relationship with the children?

Finances: Are you having financial problems? If so, what sources of help do you have available, and are you taking advantage of any of them? Have you talked with your partner about sharing responsibility for financial obligations?

Career: How are you doing at work? Are you able to concentrate, or is your work slipping? Has your career been put on hold while you try to work out this crisis? Have you buried yourself in work to forget the pain, working overtime, taking on too many assignments?

Support System: Do you have a network of family or friends who can provide emotional support or practical assistance? Are you relying on them, or have you become a recluse, withdrawing into your shell and wanting just to be left alone?

Social Activities: How is your social life in general? Do you keep yourself from get-togethers with your married friends, worried that they won't want a "fifth wheel"? Are your friends excluding you, not wanting to choose between you and your spouse because they have been friends with both of you? Do you dread weekends because there's nothing to do, or are you scheduling activities?

Spiritual: Do you have religious, spiritual, or philosophical beliefs that you draw on to help you during this difficult time? Are you part of a spiritual or religious community that sustains you? Have you been reading religious materials to build your faith and encourage personal growth?

You Can Make the Most of This Time Apart

When you separate, it often feels like everything is ending, but with hard work and determination, you can experience separation as a new beginning. Don't cave in to the temptation to end your separation prematurely, even if your partner is pressuring you to get back together. During this time apart, you have a chance to let painful memories fade; to begin to uncover the real causes of your problems; and to learn new skills that will enable you to build a base for a whole new relationship. Don't pass up this opportunity to grow from your pain. By using this time to work on yourself and your relationship, you'll have a better shot at creating a new and lasting relationship. The next chapters will show you how to make the most of your separation, maximizing your chances of affecting a successful and permanent reunion.

Questions for Reflection

1. How am I doing emotionally at this time? How am I coping physically, financially, and spiritually?

    _____

    _____

2. How can I deal with the times when I'm tempted to reconcile with my partner prematurely?

    _____

    _____

3. What are the positive aspects of being separated from my partner right now?

    _____

    _____

4. Which hurtful experiences (negative history and dysfunctional patterns of behavior) need to be healed between my partner and myself before I consider reconciling?

    _____

    _____

5. What significant parts of my own life, other than the relationship, do I need to focus on right now in order to understand more about myself and my needs?

    _____

    _____

chapter *three*

How to Detach with Love and Let Go— for Now

When you first separate, you might feel desperate to contact your partner and convince him or her that you've changed. You are willing to do almost anything to redeem the relationship. The last thing you feel able to do is let go. Yet detaching and letting go— for now—is actually helpful to your chances of ever getting back together again.

At a time when you want contact, it seems implausible, if not impossible, to back away, yet this can actually be beneficial to reconciliation. Having some space may prevent you from causing further damage during this emotional time. Space will help you gain perspective about what led to the breakup, and you will be able to start working on those things that will allow your partner to see you in a new light. In short, you need a goal to detach with love—for now.

"Are you telling me that I should just stop caring? How is that going to help me get back together with Julie?" Tom asked, reacting to the suggestion that he should detach himself from the relationship for the time being. Like most people, Tom associated detachment with giving up on the relationship. "I'm very much in love with my wife, even if we've got a lot of issues between us," he said. "I don't want to send her the message that I don't want her in my life." No one was suggesting to Tom that he give up on loving his wife. Quite the contrary: Detachment is not the same as not caring, nor is it throwing in the towel on the relationship. It is simply stepping away from the relationship for a while so as to work on the things that will help you become more emotionally stable, such as taking care of yourself and meeting your day-to-day needs.

Are You Feeling Fearful Right Now?

You probably feel lonely, have no one to talk to (or maybe you've told your story to all your friends so repeatedly they don't want to listen anymore), and perhaps you have no other interests to divert you. If you don't have close friends or have no other social outlets, you may be finding things overwhelming right now.

"I dread coming home," Tom confessed. "The apartment feels so lonely and empty without Julie. I just come in and plop down on the sofa and turn on the TV. Don't ask me what I watch; it really doesn't matter. I just keep it on for the sound, for some background noise. I work out with some guys from the office a couple of times a week, but I'm not the type of person who makes friends easily, so I don't have anyone to talk with about this other than my sister. Still, while she knows Julie and I have split up, I don't want to keep burdening her with my problems. Without Julie here, I'm just lost; I hate feeling so alone. And I fear she will find someone else and then we'll never have a chance to work things out."

Like Tom, you may be frightened by the idea of being alone and facing the future by yourself, or you may fear that unless you keep pursuing her, your partner will find someone else.

Have you and your partner discussed the terms of your time apart? If you and your partner are on good terms, talk about the boundaries of the separation. Knowing what you can expect is helpful in alleviating fear of the "unknown." For example, is the separation a few months of time-out or is it indefinite? Is there a commitment to remain faithful to each other during this time or is seeing others okay? If you have children, what arrangements are necessary for their ongoing care, as well as to lessen their fears about losing a parent? Is there an agreement in place as to who will pay the mortgage, rent, and electricity? Such guidelines, if spoken about or agreed upon can help you feel more stable and less frightened by the uncertainty of time ahead. If you are unable to put some structure around your time apart, ask if meeting with a third party such as a counselor, spiritual advisor, or mediator would be more acceptable.

Fear is a very disabling emotion. It can cause you to do things that work against you, or paralyze you and keep you from turning your attention to the work that lies ahead. It's normal to have anxiety when confronted with change, such as the first day at a new job. But fear can make you do desperate things and can prevent you from achieving the emotional stability you need so as to start doing what you must do now.

Letting Go of Fear

Fear, especially the fear of being alone, is the basis of the desperate need for attachment. There are many fears associated with the ending of a relationship: fear that you'll never get your partner back, fear that your partner will turn to someone else, fear of being alone, fear of managing on your own, fear of the unknown . . . the list goes on. These are all possibilities that your imagination can make excruciatingly vivid. But the opposite is also a possibility: You could reunite with your partner; you could make it on your own; you could find interesting new people and creative outlets; you could greatly increase your self-confidence by successfully meeting new challenges.

Another reason for letting go of fear is that it's very stressful—and while stress has a few redeeming qualities, it's generally an unpleasant feeling. On a physical level, for example, your body is thrown into a fight-or-flight state in which a whole chain of events is triggered, such as knots in your stomach and elevated blood pressure. The wear and tear from being in this constant state of heightened arousal is harmful; it depletes your body of essential vitamins and minerals. On an emotional level, fear is debilitating. For example, it's difficult to think clearly and logically. This can cause you to act in irrational ways—maybe even doing things you'll regret later.

When you detach with love, you are lessening the role of fear in controlling your actions. And you are saying to your partner in essence, "I love you, and I value you. I respect your wishes and release any desire to control you. I'm going to step back for a while to concentrate on me, doing those things that are good for me and, ultimately, good for the relationship." That's the short-term goal. The long-term goal is to improve yourself so that the two of you can grow back together in a stronger way.

Three Steps to Help You Step Back and Detach— for Now

The following three steps can help you detach with love, and let go—for now. When you follow these steps, you will find it easier to let go of your need to control the situation. And as you take the focus off your partner and put it on what you need to do at this time, you'll feel more in control of yourself and the fears that tempt you to rush into a premature reconciliation (which only lessens your chances for a successful reunion).

Step 1: Acknowledge That You Are Powerless Over Your Partner

You cannot make your partner change his feelings or make him love you. The only control you have is over yourself and your own feelings. You cannot control another person, no matter how involved you are or how much you try. Rather than being trapped in a downward spiral of thinking, "I need him, and I have to be with him," you need to be able to say, "I care about him and support him. I believe in his ability to make the best decision for himself—and I can do that for myself, as well."

When you detach with love, you acknowledge that you cannot control the other person's emotions and actions, and she is going to do what she wants to do. No matter what the final outcome is, no matter what decisions the other person makes, you have to trust that she will make the best decision for herself.

> When Tom was finally able to detach and let go, it felt as if a weight had fallen from his shoulders. He told himself, "I love Julie, but I have no control over what she chooses to do. My only control is over myself. I can let Julie know that I love her and trust in her ability to make decisions for herself. By doing so, I will also be sending the message that while I will be there for her I will also be there for me. I will be doing those things that support my loss and pain, and move forward in healthy ways, as well."

To let someone know that you believe in him this way is the strongest validation of his personhood you will ever make (and, as you will see, it has high payoffs). It takes tremendous courage and faith to tell someone that you love him enough to want whatever will make him happy, that you respect and trust him enough to know he will make the right decision—even if that means he might choose not to come back into the relationship! Paradoxical as it seems, this is a win-win situation for you. Your partner is going to find you much more desirable when you feel confident enough to make such a supportive statement than when you are needy and desperate. (This goes a long way in balancing out the power between you, something that may seem right now as if the other partner has the majority share of.)

That may be hard for you to accept right now. You may feel a need to get your partner back by demonstrating your love through pursuit and entreaties. Unfortunately, such actions demonstrate only neediness and can turn off your partner. There's something about seeing a desperate person humiliate himself that makes most of us extremely uncomfortable. The other person wants to get as far away as possible. On the other hand, showing an honest desire for what's best for the other person, as well as making healthy choices for yourself, makes her feel more loved and cherished, and creates a bond of respect for you. As you will see later on in this book, doing so becomes a real head-turner in getting your partner to show an interest in getting back together with you once again.

Step 2: Recognize That You Have Sole Responsibility for Your Well-Being and Happiness

Just as you cannot make your partner have the feelings you desire, he cannot make you happy or sad either. Your only power is over yourself; you can decide what emotions you are going to allow. If you are having problems managing your emotions right now—which is no doubt the case—do find a trusted friend or counselor to help you during this painful time. The following steps will provide more details about how to do this, but in a nutshell, this is a good time to be reading all you can find in the way of relaxation skills and personal development techniques. It's a good time to get and stay in counseling. It's a good time to journal. It's a good time to join a support group. It's a good time to get into an exercise program. In short, do those things that take the focus off "her" and place it on your own well-being.

Step 3: Focus on You—Take Care of Yourself

Right now, you are probably spending most of your time thinking about your partner, wondering what you can do to bring him back. Your concentration is on him. Shift your energies to yourself and how you can be effective. Decide on the qualities within you that you can improve. Concentrate on your own needs; nurture and develop your own inner core of being.

This is all easy to say, but more difficult to do—especially at this time. Maybe you've been taking care of yourself, but when your partner walked out the door, you stopped doing things for yourself. Know that there really is light at the end of the tunnel. Consciously say to yourself, "I'm alone now, but that's only temporary. I want to be back with my partner again. I'm going to work on reconciling by focusing on my own growth and the eventual goal of being back with my partner again." Following are some action steps you can take to better care for yourself right now.

Don't Let Your Health Suffer

Are you eating properly and getting enough sleep? At a time like this, you may be eating poorly and having sleepless nights, conscious of the empty half of the bed. If you continue this way, your physical condition will weaken, which will make it even harder to get your emotions in balance. Tell yourself you're not going to let your health suffer. Have meals with friends or invite them for dinner. Plan activities that get you out of the house. Be good to yourself. You're going to need physical and mental stamina for the work ahead of you.

One of the best things you can do for yourself right now to reduce the stress you are feeling is to exercise. Exercise will help you stay fit and sleep better. (You may want to begin by having your doctor recommend a program that's right for you.) Then, develop a regular exercise program rather than overdoing exercise when you're stressed out. Make up a schedule and stick to it. You'll feel better, sleep better, and—a great bonus—look better. You'll probably also meet people and make new friends. Perhaps you've always promised yourself to get in shape when you have the time. The time is now.

Relaxation and stress-reduction techniques may also be helpful now. You may doubt that you can relax at a time like this, but remember, relaxation is a skill; it can be acquired and practiced. Stress-reduction and relaxation techniques come in many variations, but most include deep breathing, muscle relaxation, and visualization to achieve a calming effect. For additional information, refer to the Stress Management section of the Suggested Reading list in the back of this book.

Reach Out to Others

In times of stress, one of the best things you can do is to make contact with others. Call on your family and friends for support. Surround yourself with people who are willing to listen and help you through this time, those who will help you find constructive things to do (not just talk about him!), those who inspire and uplift you, those who make you laugh and divert your mind temporarily from your problems, those who help you see the best in yourself and will not judge you as you continue the journey that lies ahead.

There is a difference between finding someone who is willing to listen and someone who can help you work through things. Right now you may feel that you want a sympathetic ear more than a counselor. Find a friend who will let you express your feelings without judging or giving advice. You might say, "Thank you for just listening and letting me get things off my chest. Later on, I might be ready for suggestions, but right now, I just need some support—someone to hear me out."

You might be feeling very lonely if you relied on your partner almost exclusively for companionship. But it's never too late to make new friends. What clubs and groups are available in your workplace? What groups and activities does your church sponsor? Sign up at a gym or the local YWCA or YMCA. Take time to be with time-honored friends as well.

Get into Counseling

When the time comes that you need more than just a shoulder to cry on or a sympathetic ear, look for a greater level of support through a therapy or support group or individual counseling. Many people shy away from counseling. Sometimes they feel ashamed of needing help; sometimes they think they should be able to solve their own problems. Perhaps you have supportive family and friends and think that, with their help, you can "get through this." But don't expect your family or your best friend to be the only kind of help and support you need right now.

We tend to think that most problems can be solved by the use of common sense, but relationship problems often go beyond the commonsense solutions that seemingly would resolve them. That's what makes them so difficult. Consciously, you may tell yourself, "I can handle this situation," but inside, a voice may be saying, "I really messed this up. If I had been a better wife, companion, lover . . . he wouldn't have left me." A trained professional can help you deal with old tapes playing in your head that lower your self-esteem to take positive action.

A therapist can also help you learn how to break away from the self-damaging patterns of communicating and behaving and learn new skills. If you grew up in a troubled household, it's likely that you need to learn more constructive ways of interacting and living with the people you love—how to communicate, how to create a loving relationship, how to be a good parent—in other words, how to function more successfully. A therapist trained in these areas can help you acquire these skills. If you're experiencing symptoms such as loss of appetite, rapid and severe weight loss, sleep disturbances, difficulty getting out of bed, inability to concentrate, loss of interest in usual activities, feelings of hopelessness, or spontaneous crying spells, you should see your family doctor immediately. Sources of information for finding a therapist include your Employee Assistance Program or personnel office at work; your spiritual advisor; your local Mental Health Association; Internet sources such as WebMD and the Yellow Pages—look under Psychologists or Marriage and Family Counselors.

Meet Your Responsibilities—One Day at a Time

In addition to coping with the stress of separation, you may have children or other family members who rely on you. At this time, when most of your energy is spent dealing with your own pain, it's important to remember those who depend on you. Children especially need help in dealing with the changes that result in parental separation, such as anger or tension in the household. Take the time to find out how their day went and to talk about the things that are bothering them. Avoid blaming your partner or making your children feel that they're caught in the middle. Reassure them that they are in no way to blame for the separation. Let them know that although the grownups are having problems, you both still love them and will continue to take care of them. Because so much else has changed, try to keep their routine as regular as possible. If there are grandparents, or other relatives or friends who can help at this time, you will want to pursue their involvement as well. You might call a child psychologist for recommended books on how to help children through separation. Several are listed in the bibliography.

If you and your partner are still in communication, another way to help yourself and your children cope with the stress of separation is for both of you to agree on a few basic guidelines for the separation. Finding a way to reach agreement in critical areas such as time with the children, arrangements for their care, and financial support for the household will relieve some of your anxiety and leave more energy for you to focus on yourself. Again, if you partner is resistant to setting some structure with you, ask if meeting with a third party such as a counselor, pastor, or mediator would be more acceptable.

Resist the Urge to "Change My Entire Life"

The steps you take to renew yourself during this time will help you feel better about yourself, and will help you increase your confidence and self-esteem. Celebrate this growth and rebirth with personal improvements that are meaningful to you. Having said that, you need to know that this is not the time to "clean house"—to get rid of your life as you knew it and to start over. This really is not the time to get a facelift, move across the country, build a new house, or make other drastic changes in your life. Do make some changes, but minor ones, and go slowly, such as getting the new hairstyle you've been meaning to try, or buying an art print or new sheets for your bed. You might rearrange the furniture or buy that new chair or couch to replace an old one. The goal is to recognize that you are growing and to celebrate it tangibly in your environment so that it will lift your spirits. Just don't "throw the baby out with the bathwater." Give yourself time to make the bigger changes.

Start a Journal

Record your thoughts and feelings every day. The goal is to get your thoughts out of your head and onto paper. This can help you see how far you've come as well as help you identify areas where you need more support. For example if you're still crying yourself to sleep after five months of separation, or you're still not able to concentrate on the day-to-day activities that make up your life, then do find a counselor who can help you feel more in control of your own life. Be completely honest about your feelings. Your journal will be an invaluable record of your growth as you look back and see the progress you've made. On those days when you think nothing you've tried has worked, you can read the journal and see that, in fact, you've come a long way. You'll find that you gain new insights into your situation as you pour out your emotions. The hardest part is getting started. Following are a few topics and questions that may help you begin taking this inventory of yourself.

Self-Worth: How do you answer the question, "Who am I?" What is your identity? What's really important in your life? What brings meaning and purpose to your life? What brings you status and respect?

Physical Appearance: What do you look like? Describe your general appearance: height, weight, hair color, eye color, figure type, attractive features, and things you'd like to improve.

Personality: Are you friendly, reserved, shy, frank, open? Do you consider yourself fun-loving, serious, spontaneous, deliberate? Do you communicate freely and easily, or do you guard your speech and choose your words carefully? Do you live for excitement, or do you prefer quiet activities?

Sexuality: Can you communicate your sexual desires, what you like and don't like, openly and honestly with the person with whom you are intimate? How would you describe your sex life with your partner? What one thing would you like to change about your sex life?

Sociability: Are you happiest in a crowd of people, or do you prefer being with a few close friends? Is it easy for you to make new friends, or do you have difficulty approaching others? Are you interested in other people, or do you prefer to be alone?

Career: What are you up to in your work world? Do you like your work? Does it challenge you? Does it offer opportunities for growth? Do you enjoy the people you work with? Do you see yourself doing the same thing next year, in five years, in ten years?

Hobbies: What do you do just for pleasure? How did you know you wanted to pursue this hobby? Do you spend as much time pursuing this interest as you would like? What other interests would you like to pursue?

Family: What's your family life like? Do you have children? Are they living with you? How is your relationship with them? Do you have family members who rally around and provide support, or are you emotionally (and perhaps physically) distant from your family?

Self-Care: Do you take good care of yourself? Are you eating well, exercising, getting adequate rest? Do you schedule and keep annual exams? What aspects of your health would you like to improve?

Home Life: Is your home a place where you can relax, nurture yourself, and escape from the stresses of the job? What one thing would you most like to change about where you live?

Spirituality: Do you believe in a Higher Power? What faith do you practice? Do your beliefs sustain and inspire you in good times and bad? What one thing would you like to know more about?

Schedule Your Activities

Because of the separation, you might have been somewhat self-critical, tending to blame yourself for things you feel you "should" have done. Don't be too hard on yourself at this time. Remember that during the early stages of separation, you may not be functioning as well as you were before the breakup. This is normal, so allow for more time to complete tasks. Don't don your "superhero" cape and try to overcompensate for your feelings right now. Relax and slow down.

Chances are that you have a lot of things on your mind other than your day-to-day activities. You may find yourself being more forgetful than usual. Just accept that, and leave yourself reminder notes on the refrigerator, in the car, and at work. Double-check your work to be sure you've finished everything. Reassure your friends, family, and supervisor that this absentmindedness is only a temporary condition and that you'll be back to normal soon. Quite probably, they'll understand and be willing to allow you the time and consideration for not being at your very best during this period.

Be careful, however, that when you relax your schedule, you don't wipe out everything, especially social activities. You need to avoid loneliness now. Keep yourself busy to limit the amount of time available to feel sorry for yourself or to dwell on the negative things that have happened (or are happening) to you. Regain control and avoid loneliness by scheduling your daily activities in detail. Notice where the empty spaces are and fill them with an activity. It doesn't have to be something strenuous; it can be as simple as a bubble bath, a walk with the dog, or an hour with a good book. The goal is to take back control of your life.

Examine your schedule right now. Does it feature the same routine things: work, driving the children to practice, chores at home?

If you're lonely, it's important to fill your days not just with routine chores but also with enjoyable or useful activities. If you have children, it's especially important that you stay balanced by arranging at least a few hours a week of fun just for yourself. If you're alone and time hangs heavy, take a class or weekend seminar, visit the art galleries in your area, or volunteer your time. In fact, volunteering is an excellent way to make you feel better about yourself; it gives you perspective about your plight. When we focus on a problem up close, it sometimes looks and feels more drastic than it really is. Becoming involved with the needs of others can make your own problem seem less severe. Your local United Way, or volunteer opportunities that appear in your newspaper, can point you to a volunteer job in almost any area you are interested in.

Weekends can be especially difficult. Make a point of scheduling your weekends well in advance. Invite someone over for brunch or dinner or to share a movie. If you have a hobby such as painting, pottery, or weaving, take some of your products to a swap meet. You might want to join a special interest group: a hiking or walking club, a folk-dance group, or a charitable organization. Many local news Web pages and newspapers print weekend activities in the Friday issue; look for something that interests you and gets you out among people.

Keep Track of Your Triumphs

Start a list of triumphs and put it up on the wall. Every day, note at least one thing that you feel proud of accomplishing. Perhaps you wanted to call your partner, just to hear his voice, but didn't. Perhaps you were able to talk with her about the children without bringing up The Other Man. Maybe you joined a lunchtime walking group, helped your child plan a birthday party, or bought some flowers to brighten your home. Write it down on your triumphs list and give yourself a mental pat on the back. Giving yourself positive verbal acknowledgment ("That was good," "I'm proud of myself") is very important. Your self-talk to a large extent determines how you feel about yourself and your situation.

There IS Light at the End of the Tunnel

Detaching is not an easy thing to do—in fact, it may be one of the most difficult things you'll ever do in your life. But you can do it—and you must do it! Remind yourself that it's the best thing for you, for your partner, and—most especially—for your relationship. Tell yourself that the dark days of your separation aren't permanent. There is light at the end of the tunnel. Be patient with yourself. Let go of your fears. Commit to working on yourself. Even though you may not think so now, this separation may be a turning point for your relationship. By "detaching and letting go—with love," you will discover hidden strengths within yourself, and feel more hopeful about your life. You'll be able to bring the best "you" to your relationship by seeing your separation as a time of renewal.

Questions for Reflection

1. What fears are preventing me from detaching with love?

   _____

   _____

2. How will I tell my partner that I am letting go—for now? How do I think he/she will react?

   _____

   _____

3. Who will I reach out to for support and companionship during this time?

   _____

   _____

4. What activities can I engage in that will soothe my heart and soul?

   _____

   _____

5. What triumphs have I achieved today? What goals do I plan to achieve tomorrow?

   _____

   _____

chapter *four*

What Do You Really Want?

You're at a turning point now. You're learning how to step back and get away from the relationship temporarily, and to focus on yourself, doing things to take care of your needs, and regaining your emotional balance. Now is the time to delve deeper and take a hard and honest look at your needs and goals. Questions such as "What do I want?" and "What should I do now?" are best answered by turning to your values. Values are the principles that serve as your guideposts for living. They express your most deeply held beliefs and play a prominent role in shaping your goals. Identifying and understanding your most important values gives you a more complete picture of what you need for your happiness. This chapter serves as the basis of a plan for reconciliation based around your needs and values; Chapter 5 will show you how to construct the plan.

What do you value? Maybe you answer like many do: by saying, love, happiness, close family, or friends. The point is that our goals stem from our values. For example, if you say, "I value education," then maybe you hold a goal such as getting a degree. Or if you value adventure, then maybe a goal would be to do something adventurous like learning to parasail or going on a safari. If you hold a value for service to others, then your goal might be to be a better parent, or to volunteer at a senior citizens' home or do some sort of activity that would serve others in your family or community.

If your goals stem from your values, your actions are in harmony with your innermost being.

When our goals conflict with our values, something within feels amiss. For example, perhaps you value honesty and integrity, but sometimes you find yourself in situations where those values are compromised. Or you may value being part of a twosome, but not want to be accountable to a partner. When too many of your deeply held values are in conflict, as often happens in a troubled relationship, you can begin to feel depressed and anxious because you are compromising your integrity.

How Are Your Values Being Expressed?

Because your values play such an important role in shaping your goals, it's important to know what you really value—as opposed to what you think you should value. This is a good time to explore how your values are being expressed in your life. Are you living according to your values, or are they being compromised to the point of making you deeply uncomfortable? How well or poorly were your values being expressed in your relationship? The more you are able to live your life according to the values you hold dear, the more fulfilling and satisfying your life will be. And the more values you share with your partner, the more satisfying your relationship will be.

What Are Your Values?

What's really important to you? Think through what living or not living according to that value in your life would mean to you. Perhaps you value independence, while a mutual relationship depends on interdependence. Do you say you want a child because your family believes that children are needed to complete a marriage, or because you want to enjoy nurturing and raising children? Do you value job security because you have been taught that it's more important to have a steady income than to take the risks that might be associated with moving from career to career? Do you value having power over others, even though you were taught that cooperation is more important? When your values are in conflict, you have to look for ways to satisfy conflicting needs or decide which values take precedence over others.

The following categories will start you thinking about your own values. As you read through the questions and answer them, you'll identify those values that you want to incorporate into your life right now. And you'll get a chance to see if, and how, they fit, or don't fit, into the relationship with your partner.

As you're going through them, ask yourself whether your first response is one that you have been taught to believe is "correct" or whether it reflects your own deeply held beliefs. Remember, there are no "right" answers. There's only what is right for you. Later in this chapter you'll get a chance to prioritize the values that are really important to you. For now, spend some time thinking about all the values you hold dear. Again, take some time to think this through. You may even want to jot down some notes for yourself, or even journal on this.

Personal Values: What individual qualities are important to me? What characteristics do I value in myself and seek out in others? How important is a good sense of humor? Loyalty? Friendship? Trust? Honesty? For myself, do I strive for adventure, good health, personal growth, peace of mind, recognition, stability?

Security Values: How important is it to me to be financially secure? Am I okay with making a lower wage as long as the work is something I enjoy? Do I "live to work" or "work to live"? Do I take financial risks or invest conservatively? Do I consider long and carefully before making large purchases, or am I an impulsive buyer?

Relationship Values: Do I want a relationship characterized by open and honest communication? Do I need a relationship in which we spend a great deal of time together, or are times apart and separate activities acceptable? Do I want to be involved in my partner's career or business? Do I want to make decisions jointly, or am I satisfied to let my partner make the best decisions for our relationship?

Partner Values: What qualities do I value in a partner? Do I want a partner who will support me in my career and be proud of my achievements? Do I require absolute fidelity, or am I willing to "look the other way" under certain circumstances? Can I accommodate a partner whose sexual needs differ significantly from my own? Do I value spontaneity and a sense of fun in my partner? Do I want a partner who will take care of me, or one who will give me some space and allow me to be independent? Do I want my partner to be honest with me at all times, even if I may not like what I hear?

Family Values: How do the needs of my children or partner weigh against my own needs? Do I want active involvement from my partner in child rearing, or am I willing to take on the major tasks? Am I strict with my children, or would I characterize my parenting style as "relaxed"? Do I treasure a close-knit family that gets together frequently, or do I prefer to keep the focus on my own immediate family? Are family traditions important to me? Am I willing to support a parent—financially, physically or emotionally—if the need arises?

Work Values: Do I think of my work as a job or as a career? Do I work primarily for the income or for the satisfaction? Do I need power and status? Do I want to be recognized for my skills? Do I seek to be an entrepreneur or to climb to the top of the corporate ladder? Or am I content with a job that allows me enough time and energy to focus on my family and friends? Do I enjoy working with people, or do I prefer to work alone?

Spiritual Values: Do I have a personal belief system or philosophy of life that inspires and sustains me? Do spiritual or religious beliefs play an important part in my life? Do I strive to live in accordance with my religious or spiritual beliefs? Is it important that my partner share my spiritual beliefs? Do I want my children raised in my religious tradition?

Setting Your Priorities

The reason to identify your values is to see if they're being expressed in your life, and to see if you're content in the way they are playing out. In the previous exercise, you made a large list of the things that are important to you. Sometimes we can be content when certain values aren't completely expressed in our lives. Other times, we're not willing to compromise. That's why it's important to prioritize which values are most important to you. The following exercise is your opportunity to go back through the previous values and identify two values in each category that are of utmost importance to you.

You'll be using these a little later on to create a well-focused plan of reconciliation, but for now, narrow your list to those two values in each category that you aren't willing to be flexible on. Note: We've given you an example for each category to get you started. In the left-hand column, we have listed one person's choices from each category. List yours in the right-hand column.

Example	Your Values
Personal Values	
1. Adventure	1. _____
2. Good health	2. _____
Security Values	
1. High salary	1. _____
2. Conservative investments	2. _____
Relationship Values	
1. Open communication	1. _____
2. Joint decision-making	2. _____
Partner values	
1. Fidelity	1. _____
2. Honesty	2. _____
Family Values	
1. Shared parenting	1. _____
2. Stable family	2. _____
Work Values	
1. Satisfaction	1. _____
2. Recognition	2. _____
Spiritual Values	
1. Attendance at place of worship	1. _____
2. Spiritual Growth	2. _____

How Well Does Your Relationship Fit Your Values?

Now that you've identified values you deem very important, ask yourself how well your relationship meshes with them. Does your relationship satisfy the values that are the most important to you? Go back to your list above and write "yes" or "no" next to each one when you consider whether your relationship supports each value. For example, if your goal is to spend more time with your young children, and your partner deems this important as well, write "yes" next to that value. If you're hoping to find more time for travel, but your partner does not like to travel, you may want to write "no" next to that value.

When you're done, take a look at how many "no" answers you wrote. How much do you find yourself compromising and accommodating—not living according to your values—to please your partner? When there's too much of a contrast between your ideals and your actions, anger, resentment, depression, or guilt can set in. If many of your ideals have been compromised in your relationship, you may want to face the issue clearly and ask yourself how many of your values you are willing to do without or modify. For example, are you willing to forgo your partner's support or validation of your career if it means achieving your value of an intact family? What if you value achievement, but your husband feels that you should spend less time on your job and more with the family? Are you willing to give up a degree of candor in your communications if it means avoiding accusations and quarrels? Is having an exciting sexual relationship a satisfactory trade-off for not sharing household responsibilities?

Sometimes it's difficult to separate out what you should want from what you do want. One way to resolve this dilemma and find out what you really value is to watch what you do, as opposed to what you say. For example, you might say, "I value honesty in my relationship," but skirt around certain issues for fear of what might happen if you confronted them openly. In that case, what you value most is maintaining the status quo in the relationship, rather than openly confronting issues that might change it—whether to improve or destabilize. Watch what you actually do; actions speak louder than words and can give you insight as to what is most important to you.

If You Need Help Finding Out What You Want

There are times when your emotions are in such a state of turmoil it's not possible to rationally analyze your needs and motivations. Long-suppressed desires often need to be uncovered to identify your true goals and effectively attain them. If you are having difficulty deciding which values are most important to you, look for help in clarifying your thinking, either in a support group or through counseling.

Some values you hold are absolute and will brook no compromise. But on many other points, there is flexibility. Your goal is to identify those values on which you are flexible and those values on which you have to stand firm for the sake of your own peace of mind and happiness. While a "perfect" relationship may not be immediately attainable, you do want one in which most of your basic needs for happiness are met. In the next chapter, we'll help you translate your values into a specific plan for reconciliation in which your most important values and needs are being met.

Questions for Reflection

1. What are the three most important values in my life?

    a. _____

    b. _____

    c. _____

2. How have my values influenced the choices I have made?

    _____

    _____

3. Which of my values conflict with my partner's values?

    _____

    _____

4. Which values am I absolutely unwilling to compromise on?

    _____

    _____

5. Which values will I give up for the sake of satisfying my partner?

    _____

    _____

chapter *five*

Getting Your Partner Back:
Creating Your "Plan of Action"

> "When a friend told me I should have a plan for getting Lynn back, I thought that sounded so manipulative," said John. "But the more I thought about it, the more it made sense. It was becoming clear that she wasn't going to come back just because I kept telling her how much I loved and needed her. In fact, it seemed to drive her away, because I sounded so desperate. The more emotional I became, the more distant she was. I realized I needed a plan to help me manage myself, a plan to put my strong emotions aside for the moment and focus on regaining my balance so that getting back together was even possible. I had to have a plan of action if I was going to do the things that would help Lynn see me in a more positive light and hopefully be interested in reconciling."

Can you relate? Did you notice that when you told your partner how much you love her and want her back, your pleas fell on deaf ears? It's unlikely that your partner will be swayed by protestations of undying love or promises that you'll try harder to do better. She may have made some temporarily encouraging gestures of kindness out of feelings of guilt for your unhappiness. But over time, invoking such feelings or displaying neediness will only serve to convince her that she was justified in leaving you. Feeling powerless makes you believe that you aren't in control of your life, lowering your self-esteem further. It's a vicious circle and a destructive one. This is another reason for having a plan that guides your actions at this time.

Devising a plan isn't just about the other person—it's also about you. It's a strategy to manage yourself and your emotions, a map that guides you in handling yourself in positive and productive ways during this time.

Setting Goals to Achieve a Plan of Action

When you want your partner back, how can you stop acting needy and desperate, or being pushy or aggressive? One way to do this is to stop focusing solely on your partner or his issues, and, instead, turn your focus on you. Dwelling on the separation won't bring your partner back. You need a concrete plan of action that will help you focus on the work to be done to make reunion possible. When you set important goals, you become much more active and purposeful. At this point, it's important that you summon up positive feelings while you work toward fulfilling your goals.

Perhaps you feel hurt, confused, angry, and lonely, and you're unsure if you even have the ability to create a plan right now. This is understandable; your self-confidence has been dealt quite a blow. This loss of confidence is another reason why it's important to be organized and focused on your objectives. Remember: Your ultimate goal is not just reconciliation, but to create a healthy relationship.

You have to know what you want before you can plan to get it. By identifying your values and assigning priority to them, you've taken the first step toward setting the goals that help you get what you want. You're taking charge of your life. Instead of reacting to events, you're becoming proactive—determining what you want to bring about for your future.

The goals will incorporate your core values, so that your relationship expresses what's important to you. For example, if you value intimacy, one goal is to be able to communicate openly so that you can achieve it. A goal is the bridge that takes you from merely wishful thinking ("I wish I had her back"), to actions that help you achieve it ("When my husband and I talk by phone, I'm not going to be negative or hang up on him").

Without a plan, you have little control over what happens. Right now, you may think that your partner is the only one who holds the key to what will happen. You may feel that you have very little control over what occurs in your relationship; after all, he's the one who decides whether he'll come back to you or not. It's true that your partner will make that decision because he controls his life. But you are the one who can control your life. A plan of action gives you the means to regain control of your life. You have something solid to hold onto when events are spinning all around you. Something to remind you that you're not helpless—there are things you can do.

Guidelines for Setting Goals

Planning is critical at this stage of separation because it enables you to build the bridge to reconciliation. Goals let you plan for the bigger picture by setting tangible tasks that can spell the difference between wishful thinking and bringing about a desired outcome. But you'll want to focus your energy, your actions, on those that have the highest payoff in moving you toward getting what you want. Following are some principles to keep in mind as you start setting your goals.

Find Your Balance

When you think about goals right now, one probably seems to be at the center of everything: to get back together with your partner. As we said earlier, reunion should not even be your main goal at this point. Your number-one objective right now should be taking care of yourself. Attend to your physical, emotional, social, and spiritual needs, many of which have probably been somewhat neglected. Are you attending to your:

- **Physical needs**—eating healthy, getting enough rest, and exercising?

- **Emotional needs**—reading self-help books, keeping a journal so that you can record your feelings and see progress, listening to music that uplifts your mood?

- **Social needs**—spending time with good friends, joining an interest group, taking a class in something that intrigues you?

- **Spiritual needs**—meditating, reading inspirational books, joining a worship group?

If you answered no to any of these, start attending to them today. If you find it just too difficult to get motivated to care for yourself, you may want to find a counselor or therapist to help you get through this stress-filled time.

Set Goals That Are Important to YOU

It's important that your goals be what you truly want rather than what others recommend. For example, you don't have to pursue a college degree simply because your spouse wanted to earn an advanced degree. And while you're spending more time with friends (who perhaps are all advising you to start seeing others, to take a night course or a trip around the world), now is not necessarily the best time to tackle such things. Think about what you want to do that is good, comforting, and helpful for you right now. Work toward those goals that are meaningful to you, that make you a better and stronger person; this will, in the end, be very instrumental in your partner seeing you in a new and positive light. This will also be helpful in your goal to reconcile with your partner.

Set Realistic and Achievable Goals

Believing in yourself may be the most difficult part of goal setting for you right now, so make realistic goals that you can achieve. For example, rather than setting a goal like "Have dinner with Michael this weekend" when Michael hasn't spoken to you recently and doesn't return your calls, a more realistic goal might be to "Have Michael taking my calls six weeks from now." If your goals are overwhelmingly difficult, you will only become frustrated or, even worse, give up on bringing your goals to fruition.

Take It One Step at a Time

Even though your ultimate goal is reconciliation, take it one step at a time. At first, set yourself the task of simply regaining the sense that you're going to be okay and are more ready to start a plan of action. Once you start feeling as if you've regained some of your personal strength, you can venture into other areas. For example, if you have initiated contact with your partner via note or telephone, your next step might be to arrange to meet informally in an unthreatening environment that does not have a "date" feeling so that you can share with her what you're doing for yourself. Slowly but surely, as you meet each goal, you'll gain confidence. You will be able to see that you are making progress toward your ultimate desire.

Put Your Goals in Writing

Committing your goals to writing (moving them from your head onto paper) gives structure to what you're attempting to achieve. The task of writing them moves them from wishful thinking to a concrete plan—something you can readily do something about. For example, writing on your calendar, "I will call or send Michael a note by the end of the week" is more specific than thinking in your head, "I sure wish Michael knew that I was doing all these great things for myself." Written goals are tangible, confidence-inspiring targets that you can see come to life.

Make a Timetable

Having a timetable keeps you on track so that you can follow your plan's progress. In scheduling targets involving your partner, such as time with the children, be flexible and realistic. Rather than writing down, "Have Michael wanting to move back in by Christmas," you may want to say, "Have Michael commit to picking up the kids and taking them to school each week by Christmas." Having a timetable keeps you on track so that you can follow your plan's progress, and it motivates you when things seem to be slowing down or even stalling. It takes persistence and determination to achieve your goal—so give yourself that time. Having an unrealistic timetable will only add to your stress and can even create feelings of hopelessness or despair.

Create Goals That Reflect Your Values

With that in mind, it's time to turn each of the values you identified in Chapter 4 into goals. These goals fall into two categories: broad goals that reflect your core values; and small, achievable goals that are stepping-stones toward achieving your broad goal. Start with one small, achievable goal for each large goal that reflects your values. When you achieve it, continue onward in that area to learn more, or move on to another goal. Remember, every improvement you make in one area will have a positive impact on all the others. The following table is an example to help get you started.

One Person's Values and Goals

Personal Values	Personal Goals
1. Adventure	1. To go scuba-diving
Small goal: Research facilities that offer scuba-diving certification.	
2. Good Health	2. To lose fifty pounds
Small goal: Call Weight Watchers to see where I can attend a meeting.	

Security Values	Security Goals
1. Higher Salary	1. To get a raise this year
Small goal: Take a computer certification class to improve my job skills and increase my eligibility for a raise.	
2. Conservative Investments	2. To invest only in ventures that offer little risk
Small goal: Review my portfolio to see if any of my investments need to be redirected into less risky ventures.	

Relationship Values	Relationship Goals
1. Open Communication	1. To discuss my fears with my partner without being ridiculed
Small goal: Write a letter to my partner sharing my need for open communication.	
2. Joint decision-making	2. To enlist my partner in making decisions about our finances
Small goal: Consult with a financial planner who can help us plan our financial future.	

Partner Values	Partner Goals
1. Fidelity	1. To accept no less than absolute fidelity from my partner and the peace of mind that comes from knowing that he wants to be faithful
Small goal: Sign up for a personal growth workshop to strengthen my convictions.	
2. Honesty	2. To learn with my partner to be totally open with each other
Small goal: Find a counselor who teaches communication skills.	

Family Values	Family Goals
I. Shared Parenting	I. To make child rearing a joint activity, with my partner sharing the responsibility (I don't want to be a "single parent" in my marriage.)

Small goal: Research parenting groups that we could attend together.

2. Stable Family	2. To make our family the most stable and secure thing in our lives, and have our children feel safe and loved

Small goal: Plan a "family night" once a week.

Work Values	Work Goals
I. Satisfaction	I. To help people through work

Small goal: Join a professional group that does community work.

2. Recognition	2. To achieve recognition for being productive

Small goal: Take on a challenging project at work that is important to my boss.

Spiritual Values	Spiritual Goals
I. Attendance at my place of worship	I. To participate more fully at my place of worship

Small goal: Join a membership class at my place of worship.

2. Spiritual Growth	2. To grow in knowledge and awareness, searching for greater understanding

Small goal: Read from inspirational writings every night before going to sleep.

Identifying the Obstacles to Your Goals

You have already taken an essential step in planning for your reunion, and that is to identify what's most important to you so that you can decide how to achieve it. The next step is to find out what things might stand in your way—and how to remove them. Here are some typical obstacles you may encounter.

Negative Self-Talk

You can quiet that little negative voice that tries to sabotage your efforts. Telling yourself things such as, "He'll never come back," only robs your confidence. When your thinking mode turns negative, replace the negative self-talk with positive self-talk. Use affirmations such as, "I'm staying the course," "I'm feeling better about myself, and my life is looking better," "I'm just going to keep working my plan." Repairing your relationship and creating a new one may not be easy, but it helps to stay positive.

Fear of Committing to Your Goals

Now that you've identified your goals, commit to reaching them. If you're afraid of taking the first step, remind yourself that achieving your goals moves you closer and closer to a more fulfilling life and a possible reunion with your partner. Your plan reflects the things that are important to you. Your commitment is the fuel that focuses you and gives your plans a chance to succeed. Believe in yourself and your ability to achieve your goals.

Impatience

Things didn't go from bad to worse overnight, and it will take time to turn the situation around. Be patient and willing to invest that time. Wanting to either "reconcile right now, or just get it over with and end it," might cause you to consider walking away without giving yourself a fair chance. Work your plan and follow constructive steps toward your goal. When you have setbacks, or when things don't go as planned, regroup and begin again. Keep your eye—and heart—on the goal.

Fear of Being Ridiculed

It's uncomfortable when others think you're crazy for wanting your partner back—especially if that person treated you unkindly or was unfaithful. But this is your life. If this is what you want, then keep a positive attitude about your goals and do not let them be undermined by the opinion of others.

Fear of Failure

What if you put in all this effort, turn a deaf ear to those who think your plan is foolish, follow through on all the steps, and still don't succeed? It can and may happen. But you will have the satisfaction of knowing that you followed your heart, worked a good plan, and gave it your best effort. In other words, you did all you could. Best of all, you've made an enormous investment in yourself that has rewarded you with increased feelings of self-worth and a renewed self-confidence. Your efforts have taken you to the next level and made you a stronger and better person for your next relationship.

Visualize the Benefits of Achieving Your Goals

Imagine all the good things that will come as a result of accomplishing your goals. Create a mental image of your new and improved life one year from now. Think of what you want, and make your visualization as detailed and vivid as possible. Perhaps you see both of you enjoying the things you used to do, like a walk in the park or lunch at the coffee shop. Or imagine sitting at the dinner table as a family again. By focusing on your desired end result, your subconscious mind will work with you to bring it about. Some excellent books describing the use of imagery to achieve your goals can be found in the Suggested Reading section at the back of this book.

You Can Do It!

The ancient adage, "A journey of a thousand miles starts with a single step" is absolutely true. Whether your goal is to return to college to fulfill your degree or to rebuild your relationship, focus on what you can do now. What is the first small step? Whether it's to look in the telephone book for the college admissions office telephone number, or to sign up for a communication class, take that first step now. It's the step that leads you to fulfilling your goal.

Questions for Reflection

1. What am I doing to attend to my physical, emotional, social and spiritual needs?

    _____

    _____

2. What tasks can I write on my calendar for this week that will take me closer to reaching my goals?

    _____

    _____

3. What goals do I find the most challenging to meet?

    _____

    _____

4. What obstacles do I need to remove to achieve my goals?

    _____

    _____

5. How will I share my values and goals with my partner?

    _____

    _____

chapter *six*

Are You Ready to Reconcile?

Throughout this book, the emphasis has been placed on you. Our goal has been to encourage you to evaluate your life, to look inward and decide what is working and what isn't. Knowing yourself well enough to determine what you need and want, both in the relationship and for yourself, gives you a much better chance of reconciling into a relationship that endures.

In previous chapters, we talked about how to regain control of your life and work toward reconciliation through such steps as identifying your values and then setting goals aimed at achieving them. Although you love your partner and want to be together again, you've accepted responsibility for your own life. You've examined your ability to communicate on a more intimate level and developed a plan for focusing your emotions into constructive actions. In other words, you are loving your way back into the relationship.

Don't Rush Back!

You may have decided that if the relationship is to work for you, some important changes will have to be made. Before you consider reunion, make certain that the needed changes have been instituted or are well on their way to being made so that you've created the foundation for the type of relationship you want. Don't let your need for love and security rush you into a situation for which you are not emotionally prepared. If you're still waking up in the middle of the night feeling anxious and hurt, it might be tempting to get back together just to ease that pain and loneliness. Work through your pain, and don't consider getting back together until you are feeling emotionally strong and healthy. The times when you don't feel strong and you long for your partner may lead you to consider a premature reunion. If you find yourself lapsing to a previous stage, go back and reread the chapter in this book that applies. Be sure that you are ready to move forward. For example, unexpressed, pent-up anger may cause you to lash out at your partner and destroy your chances for a successful reconciliation. This does not mean that you should repress your feelings, but rather that you need to express them in a way that does not undermine the relationship.

"Two years after Jack left me for another woman," Eileen told us, "he came back filled with apologies and saying his leaving was the biggest a mistake he had ever made. He said he wanted to put our marriage back together, and hoped I did too. As much as I still loved him, and even though there was a part of me that wanted him back, I still had tremendous anger over his betrayal. But despite all the walls I put up, Jack stayed true to his goal of winning me back. Coupled with our trying to work things through, I was also going through some very difficult times with health and family issues, but Jack was always there when I needed something—quietly doing what needed to be done and never demanding anything. He was such a good friend to me throughout those challenges. My heart just melted one day, and I said, 'I think we can be together again. Do come back home.' I haven't regretted this decision. Our bond is stronger now than it's ever been. I feel that since we've made it through this, we can make it through anything now. I really trust the new relationship we've created."

Each heart takes its own time to heal. Despite Eileen's love for Jack, she knew she was not ready to reconcile as soon as he was. For one, she had too much anger to work through. Fortunately, Jack's plan to win Eileen back included waiting things out, which gave her the time and space to heal. Jack also persevered in working toward repairing the damage done by his betrayal by being a loyal friend whose devotion never wavered.

Whether you're working toward reconciliation alone, or whether your partner shares the same goal, you'll want to evaluate your readiness to be back in the relationship. Have confidence. You possess many of the resources needed to mend your relationship. Looking inward and gaining personal strength helps you deal with crisis in a way that increases the possibility of a successful reconciliation. Rather than becoming immobilized by loneliness or giving up on your relationship, you can see it as an opportunity to rethink what you really want and need in your life. As you find your own center of power, you'll be in a better position to reunite successfully.

How to Know When the Time Is Right to Reconcile

After all the hard work you've done getting to this point, be careful that you don't rush back prematurely. Being ready to love your way back into the relationship includes being willing to take things slowly. This is especially difficult to do if you're still at the stage when every fiber of your being is looking for love, when you lie awake at night just wanting to be held by your partner. So how do you know when the time is right? Is there a best time to get back together with your partner? What will work for you? Following are some guideposts to help you make a more logical, well-reasoned decision.

Are the Old Issues Resolved?
You have taken a long look at how you handled yourself during the separation. Now it's time to determine what problems created the separation in the first place. Up to this point, the main focus of concern was your own emotional well-being. As you worked on yourself, some

of the roots of your difficulties may have become apparent. Now you are more empowered, and you are ready to examine them.

Begin this analysis by listing the symptoms and probable causes (if you can identify them) of the problems leading to the break-up of your relationship. A symptom is the specific behavior that disturbs you. The causes are the events or conditions that fostered the symptom(s). For each symptom, write down what you perceive as the cause and what changes need to be made. Here are some examples:

> *Symptom:* We never had any special time for just the two of us.
>
> *Cause:* We were always with a crowd of her friends.
>
> *Changes I Would Like:* We would have at least two nights a month that would be our special "date" nights.

> *Symptom:* He refused to accept any responsibility for child rearing, thinking that was my job as a wife and mother.
>
> *Cause:* His mother was in sole charge of child rearing.
>
> *Changes I Would Like:* He would spend more time with the children, giving them their baths each night and reading them bedtime stories.

Dividing your list into symptoms, causes, and the changes that need to be made will give you a good insight into what needs to be done in the relationship and whether you can expect those symptoms to be resolved. Remember, symptoms are just outgrowths of causes, and in order for the relationship to improve, you need to understand the underlying causes, as well as know what changes in behavior you need.

Look at your list carefully. Have the problems been resolved? Some you might have solved yourself just by becoming more capable. For example, if you had financial problems and you have since gotten a raise, that's one problem that might seem less urgent now. If your spouse had a drinking problem, but has been sober for six months and is regularly attending AA meetings, you might feel more confident about his diligence for sobriety. Some of the problems may have resolved themselves, at least for the time being, without any help. Perhaps your last child went off to college, cooling down the arguments you used to have over curfews and car use. Maybe the promotion you were working toward—initiating a furious battle over how much time you already give to your career rather than to your family—went to someone else.

Your partner might have solved some problems on her own, too. She might have decided that your relationship was more important than spending long hours at the office. Maybe she changed to a less stressful job and is therefore less irritable, or she is learning to be more open in her communication. If the problems seem to have been mostly resolved, that's wonderful, but be cautious. Make sure your new foundation is solid. Remember: Insist on the patterns of behavior that work for the relationship.

Have You Learned New Patterns of Behavior?

Despite Penny's yearning for a close-knit family life, Josh spent most weekends golfing with friends and one or two nights a week at his favorite club, often not coming home until late. Before their twins were born, Penny had often been able to accompany him, but with two toddlers she was no longer able to.

Penny was a devoted mother and wanted Josh to stay home more often now that they had children, but he kept up his socializing just as he had before the twins were born. It hurt her that Josh was so uninterested in being a parent. She worried about the eventual effect of a distant father on her sons, and they argued constantly about Josh's need to come and go as he pleased.

Penny said, "I nagged him until I was blue in the face about his responsibilities to the boys. But the more I nagged, the worse things got. Finally, we separated. I began to see that my nagging behavior was not getting the response that I needed from Josh. I learned new methods for communicating and began to express my concerns to Josh in a nonaccusatory way. Finally, I feel that Josh understands my need for him to be a more involved parent. Changing my style of communication made a huge difference. Josh now realizes how much his home and family mean to him. He and I have been talking about how he can spend more time with the twins, as well as how he and I can spend more alone time together. Since we've reconciled, things have been great. We're both working really hard at meeting each other's needs and devoting quality parenting time to our sons."

What to Do When Little or Nothing Has Changed

What if problems have remained the same, improved only superficially, or even gotten worse? What do you do then? Idyllic as a reunion may seem, if the original problems are not well on the way to being resolved, you're going right back into the frying pan. No matter how much you love each other, the same fights and battles are going to erupt. If nothing has happened, the most romantic weekend won't change the basics—you still have the same relationship that didn't work.

What will you do about it? Will you reunite, knowing that the identical situation exists? "Honey, come back to me and we can work things out; I promise I'll stop losing my temper." Promises of change after the reunion are rarely fulfilled. Even if your partner means (or thinks he means) every word, don't count on anything to change after you get back together if there haven't been significant changes before. Change takes more than words; it takes determination, action, and time. If the separation, painfully shocking as it was, was not enough of a wake-up call to motivate change, your (or his) return certainly will not.

Returning to the same situation completes the cycle in which you and your partner fall back into the same dysfunctional behaviors. Change is much harder when reunited than when apart. That's one of the reasons we keep suggesting that you use this separation time to grow as a person, regain your self-esteem, and strengthen your confidence.

If the situation does not change, you'll have to do a great deal of soul-searching. You may have to decide whether to settle for the old relationship, with all its problems, or whether to end it.

Should You Compromise Your Values?

By this time, you know yourself much better than you did before the separation. You have identified what's important to you. You have also identified the problems in the relationship and decided which ones conflict with your values. Now you have to decide just how important being able to live your values in the relationship is to you, and whether you are willing to compromise on some of them or even forgo them entirely.

Few things are black and white. On many points, you and your partner will be able to work out adjustments so that the needs of both of you can be met. Yet, when it comes to your core values, to those things that define who you are and how you expect to live your life, you must be willing to be strong. If you insist on fidelity, you may have to pay the price right now of being lonely for a while longer. If you decide you can't wait to have your partner back, you may have to pay the price of living with the fact—knowing that she's being unfaithful. Such choices are not easy to make. Take your time before you make your decision and be sure that you understand the consequences fully.

How Much Are You Willing to Compromise?

"I always thought that if I found out my husband was cheating on me, it would mean the end," said Karen. "But when he actually headed for the door, I found out how much I was willing to compromise. I was eager for us to stay together and work through this. I had to find a way to go beyond infidelity, to heal, forgive, and move on in order to have Jim back."

Like Karen, you may have to rethink and come to terms with value-laden issues and determine if you can do what is necessary to reunite with your partner. Can you make a complete shift in the way you see things? Are you willing to do what it takes to go beyond the pain? For example, if your spouse was unfaithful, can you see infidelity as a symptom of a relationship that wasn't working, or as a misguided attempt to escape from a personal problem that your partner was experiencing? Will you dwell on the infidelity or the lack of companionship, and let it cost you the relationship? How often will you forgive and forget?

Can You Wait It Out?

Making change takes time. Suppose that you are absolutely unwilling to reunite while your partner is still gambling. Quitting is only the first step. He still will need to get help by attending Gamblers Anonymous or other support groups, or by seeing a therapist who specializes in addictions. In addition, he probably needs financial counseling, a schedule of regular payments to his creditors, and perhaps employment counseling. All of these take time. You need to decide whether you are willing to reunite at the beginning of his program or prefer to wait until some measurable progress has been made.

If your partner seems to be making a sincere effort or is actively seeking help, you may decide that good faith is enough and return. You may also want to join a support group for partners and families of addicts such as Alanon or Co-Dependents Anonymous in order to gain information and understand your role in the addiction process. Or you may decide to stay apart until she has been in recovery for six months or a year. Just be sure you make an informed choice. Again, don't feel you have to do this on your own; seeing a counselor is a good way to get the support you need now, as well as serve as a good sounding board to help you think—and work—things through.

Have You Reclaimed Your Life?

You've identified your values and set goals to get what you really want. Now you're determining whether you have come far enough and are stable enough to be ready for reconciliation at this time. You've considered whether the old problems have been resolved and what still needs to be done. You've decided what to do if little has changed. You've decided how much to compromise and on what. By now, you're recognizing that your decisions revolve around you and tie in with how much you understand yourself and what you want out of life. At this stage there are some very important questions to ask yourself.

How to Know If You've Regained Your Equilibrium

Are you in control of your emotions now, or are your emotions controlling you? Regardless of who left whom or why, when you and your partner separated your life changed dramatically. Suddenly, the familiar routine was no longer the same. You might have found yourself avoiding friends, worried that they wouldn't want a "fifth wheel" around. Perhaps you abstained from social activities or avoided familiar places because you didn't want to break into tears. You might have had difficulty at work. You probably spent more time than usual with your children, giving them support and drawing strength from them. Or, maybe you devoted less time to them, even neglected them. The commonplace, everyday activities that provided structure changed—perhaps drastically shattering the familiar comfort of your life.

Things are different when you are suddenly "single" again, or a "single parent." At the beginning of the separation, your world was reeling. Now, the question is: Are you on solid ground again? Have you reestablished most of your old routine, or built a new one that is comfortable for you? Have you regained your equilibrium and stabilized your life? One way to find out is to ask yourself the following questions.

1. Have I regained my balance? Can I make it through a day without crying or having other emotional outbursts? Have I developed some internal self-control that allows me to face the world and function in my daily life? Do I have a coping system that lets me manage even on the worst days?

2. Are my children doing okay? Have their lives gone back to normal as much as possible? Are they playing with their friends, getting their schoolwork done, dealing with the loss of their other parent? Are they able to talk about their father or mother without becoming emotionally upset?

3. Am I dealing well with my children? Have I learned not to criticize their father or mother in front of them? Am I refraining from expecting them to be my sole emotional support and not leaning on them more than they can handle? Am I able to normalize their lives as much as possible and treat them the same way I did before the separation, being neither too demanding nor too indulgent?

4. Am I letting my friends help me? Do I allow them to give me comfort and support in their own way, without resenting their efforts or being too demanding? Do I allow myself to be vulnerable in front of them?

5. Can my friends still count on me? Am I back to equal friendships, giving (nearly) as much as I am taking? Am I thinking about them and their needs rather than only concentrating on my concerns? Am I willing to go out with couples who are still together, and accept the possibility they love me for myself, not just as half of a couple?

6. Am I maintaining healthy habits? Am I eating properly, sleeping well, and exercising regularly? Am I taking care of and pampering myself when necessary on those "blue" days?

7. Am I accepting occasional lapses (such as the day I overdid the chocolates and skipped going to the gym)? Do I allow myself to fail once in a while without being too hard on myself? Do I recognize that there are plateaus, and that I'm not a bad person if I don't improve for a while?

8. Am I in control financially? Have I changed my spending habits to reflect my new financial situation? Have I stopped splurging just to punish him (if he's paying the bills) or to make myself feel better? Am I living a lifestyle I can afford?

9. Am I planning my financial future wisely? Am I budgeting my money, balancing my bank account, informing myself on financial issues?

10. Is my job going well? Am I functioning at the same level I was at before the breakup, or very close to it? Have my coworkers stopped giving me a little extra leeway because of my situation and begun expecting me to contribute as usual? Am I doing so? Have I settled back into the work routine?

11. Am I back to planning for the future in my job? Am I looking forward to next week, next month, next year? Do I have career goals that I am striving toward? Have I begun to look ahead at new possibilities?

12. Am I more self-reliant? Do I know that I am able to take care of myself? Do I deal with events in my life without feeling that I need to call on my partner or depend on my family? Do I respect myself and my abilities enough to know that I am able to handle most situations?

13. Am I clear about what I want and need in a relationship? Have I examined my strengths—fortifying those I already possess

and developing new ones? Do I have more self-confidence now than I did when we broke up?

These are all important questions, and you'll need to address them before you consider reconciliation. They're phrased so that the more "yes" answers you have, the more equilibrium you've regained, and the better your chances are of a successful reconciliation. Almost certainly there are a number of areas in which you are still unsteady, because regaining your equilibrium to the point where you are ready to reconcile takes time. If you go through these questions and feel that you are not yet sufficiently stable, you may want to reconsider an immediate reconciliation. It's vital that you be secure in yourself before you try to get back together. Just as you need time to recover and be strong if you've had a physical injury—you need time to recover from an emotional one. You want to go back into the relationship feeling secure that what you're doing is right for you.

And that's what your partner needs from you, too. Earlier in the book we discussed how being overly dependent and clinging can actually drive your partner away. No one wants to shoulder the burden of someone else's emotional health—it will either frighten her away or give her a sense of power over you that can lead to problems later. Remember: No one can take power from you; only you can give it away. Once you have reached emotional equilibrium, you become more desirable in your partner's eyes as a person who is in control of his own life.

Susan found this out after twenty-one years of marriage to Robert. Susan had three grown children, a good home, and what she thought was a stable marriage—that is, until Robert began womanizing. Unable to cope with the betrayal of infidelity, she left her husband. Though immobilized at first by feelings of failure and betrayal, Susan in time renewed her priorities and reorganized her life. First, she moved to another state to be near her mother, whose health was failing. Deciding she needed to improve her career qualifications, she found a job at a community college that offered a suitable program. Along the way, her self-confidence blossomed and she became more confident and—in Robert's eyes—much more desirable. Four years later, Robert decided he was completely unwilling to lose Susan for good. He and Susan began communicating on a deeper level, and Robert agreed to work on the problems that led to his betrayal of Susan. Telling her he wished to create a new life with her, he began wooing her again.

Susan still loved Robert and, confident that they had resolved the issues that led to their break-up, she took him back. She had a greatly increased sense of self-respect and self-confidence that allowed her to communicate her concerns clearly. The two have begun a business together and are completely committed to their relationship and to each other. Susan has never been happier and no longer fears that Robert will be unfaithful again. It was a harrowing ordeal, but in the end, things turned out pretty well. Susan says, "I have a 'new' relationship with the man I love, and I've developed a new relationship with me, as well!"

You Can Do It!

Moving toward reconciliation presents both hope and fear: You hope that things will be better this time, yet you fear that the destructive old patterns will reassert themselves. If you've developed your confidence and self-esteem, put your priorities in order, and learned new ways of interacting, you have the ingredients of a successful reunion. Now that you know you're ready to reconcile, the question is whether you and your partner, as a couple, are ready to come back together again—something we'll help you examine in the next chapter.

Questions for Reflection

1. What positive changes have occurred in my partner that convince me our problems have been resolved? Are there still changes to be made?

   _____

   _____

2. What new behaviors have I adopted that will lead to a more successful reunion with my partner?

   _____

   _____

3. Have I allowed enough time to convince myself that my partner's changes are permanent? If not, what time frame will I need to feel more confident?

   _____

   _____

4. Have I regained my equilibrium? Do I feel more in control of my life and my emotions?

   _____

   _____

5. How optimistic do I feel about the future with my partner? What steps will I take to continue working toward reconciliation?

   _____

   _____

chapter *seven*

Are We Ready to Reconcile?

In the previous chapter, we focused on you—how you were feeling about yourself and how you were gaining a better understanding of your needs and goals at this juncture in life. In this chapter the attention is on the "we" of the relationship.

Understanding your past and present needs can help you see how much you each have changed, and help you gain a better understanding of how those changes affect your partner and the relationship as a whole.

Use this newfound information to better understand yourself and your partner. When your needs change, your partner might not view that positively. If your partner liked that you were dependent on him when you first married, and now you are quite independent, he may feel threatened. Of course, the opposite could be true. Maybe she likes that you no longer smother her with your need for attention as you did at the beginning of the relationship.

You can also use this information to better answer the question: "Are my partner and I both ready to start building a new relationship together?"

As you consider this, think of your relationship as having three parts: you, your partner, and the relationship itself. Whatever decisions you make from now on must consider all three. Your relationship, while being made up of three separate "selves," should be focused enough and loving enough to have a single-minded heart. So while the emphasis in this chapter is on both of you, it's important now that the two of you take into consideration the impact of your individual actions on each other and on the relationship as a whole.

Marcy and George exemplify a couple that were first attracted because they filled certain needs for each other. But when Marcy's needs began to change, George felt threatened by the "new woman" his wife had become. Separation followed. Let's look at George and Marcy's story throughout this chapter to see how it is possible for a relationship to survive—even thrive—when the needs of one or both partners change.

Why Did You Choose This Person?

"I hope we can just enjoy ourselves tonight without bickering," Marcy thought, as she and George got ready to spend an evening with friends. It was an evening they were both looking forward to, but as they were getting dressed another of their all-too-frequent arguments erupted. As Marcy later told her friend Jessica, "George began making one of his 'just kidding' comments about my 'waistband challenge' again. He seems to enjoy getting a reaction out of me. His digs are really stretching my patience, really getting under my skin. I hate how annoyed we make each other."

George had his own reaction: "What happened to the woman I married? She used to care a lot about what I thought. But ever since she became a partner in the travel company, it's like I'm invisible. If the phone rings, even if we're in a conversation, it takes priority. Her whole life is about that damn career of hers! I wonder why she bothers staying married."

The conversation was characteristic of Marcy and George's interactions before their separation. Both had become disillusioned by the biting tone and accusations always evident in their conversations. It seemed to both of them that neither could do anything right. That George saw Marcy's work as the center of her life was in fact his way of saying that he was angry that his wife needed him less and less. And it was true—Marcy did need him less. As she grew more confident, she began to rely on herself instead of maintaining her earlier dependence on George. The culprit was not the much-needed self-confidence she had gained, but rather that the two of them failed to understand or discuss how this change affected each of them and their relationship. Letting digs rather than discussions do the communicating, the discord felt on both sides slowly began to undermine the relationship.

Like George and Marcy, no doubt you and your partner's needs have changed since you first got together. It can be really helpful to ask yourself: In what ways have you each changed, and in what ways (positive and negative) have those changes influenced, affected, and changed the relationship? Although our core values usually remain the same, our needs keep evolving as we go about life—learning, growing, and changing.

In relationships, change may be complementary, or it may cause conflict. Let's take a closer look at how our needs come about, and how we change when one or more are fulfilled. Marcy provides a good example of a woman who entered marriage with certain needs, but when she began to grow and became more "comfortable in her own skin," she no longer relied on her husband to fulfill her needs. This changed the dynamic of their relationship, causing tension and disappointment to consume them.

Growing up, Marcy was a sensitive and shy girl. Although comfortable in small groups, she felt overshadowed by her vivacious older sister, Angela, who was usually the center of attention. Marcy got used to being number two—a follower rather than a leader.

When she met George, she liked his super-confident attitude, and especially appreciated his take-charge approach to life. In the early years of their marriage, Marcy let George make the decisions and enjoyed that he took the lead. It felt comfortable to her because she was already accustomed to taking a secondary role in a relationship, as she did with her sister. But Marcy changed over the years as she distanced herself from her sister and began to come into her own in her professional life. As Marcy was given more and more responsibilities at the corporate travel agency where she worked, she gained leadership skills and her self-confidence grew. This newfound confidence carried over into her marriage. Marcy requested George's opinion less frequently and began making more decisions on her own—one of which was to plan a weeklong girls' ski trip to Aspen.

As George grew up, he was constantly compared unfavorably to his sister, who excelled academically and in sports and had many friends. George, in contrast, had difficulty with schoolwork and little interest in sports and was constantly belittled by his family for not measuring up. When Marcy came into his life, her shyness and dependence on him made him feel important and needed. He found security in someone else's dependence on him. It propped up his ego to be in charge. When he met Marcy, he was gratified by her attention—and liked it that she deferred to him. He told everyone that this was a woman he was comfortable with. Because Marcy needed him, he felt strong and assured. But as Marcy started to gain confidence and relied less on George, he felt his position slipping away. George had been secretly stewing about Marcy's independence for nearly a year. The final blow came when Marcy announced that she had arranged a weeklong ski trip to Aspen with her girlfriends. George exploded. To him the trip symbolized everything that had gone wrong between them. The incident triggered a major argument, and the couple separated.

Adapting to Changing Needs

George was hurt and angry when Marcy told him she felt suffocated in the relationship and resented his control. When Marcy moved out, George, who was desperate to save his marriage, sought counseling, hoping to find some way to bring her back. It took several sessions during which he raged about Marcy's "self-centeredness and lack of commitment to the relationship" before he was able to acknowledge that he had a need to feel powerful and competent—a need that had been filled by Marcy's former dependence.

Over the next few months with his therapist, George began to work through old issues regarding his own lack of self-confidence. He realized that it wasn't Marcy's job to fill his need to feel important. It was his responsibility to find new ways of meeting his needs. Through counseling, he faced his fears, and learned new behaviors and ways of viewing himself that bolstered his self-image. With practice, he gained confidence and started making friends and building a new social life for himself. He also enrolled in a management course that would open opportunities for promotion. Marcy and George continued to work on their relationship during their separation. Marcy's more confident self no longer threatened George, as he had found new ways of bolstering his own self-confidence without relying on Marcy. And Marcy felt freer to be herself—the stronger, more independent person she had become. Almost a year after their separation, George and Marcy are happily back together.

"What Happened to the Woman I Married?"

Marcy and George were wrestling with a natural "problem" so many couples face—adjusting to your changing needs and your partner's changing needs. Everyone goes into a marriage or a relationship with certain needs. One person may be looking for a feeling of belonging, another for security, and a third for the intimacy of a committed relationship. But our needs change over time: No one is ever "still the same person" you married. In this case, Marcy was once content with letting George make all the decisions without much regard for her own preferences. Marcy was looking for someone who took control—until she learned she could make decisions and be a leader, as well. As Marcy's self-confidence grew, she was less willing to look to George for reassurance and approval.

As Marcy and George discovered, you cannot look to another person to fill all your needs. You can enhance each other's lives—but you cannot live someone else's life. When George and Marcy went on their separate paths to build their own individual lives, they found they had the power to fulfill their individual needs. They came to the realization that your partner can't make you happy; he or she can only add to your happiness. It was at that point that they were able to get back together again in a mutually satisfying relationship.

What Needs Did You Bring to the Relationship?

As George and Marcy came to realize, your needs are your core requirements for happiness. They are the deep-seated desires, reflecting who you are and what you value, that you bring into a relationship. Although needs vary, most fit into one or more basic categories: physical, financial, emotional, familial, intellectual, and spiritual. Regardless of whether you're separated, currently having problems, or are back together after having been apart, think about the needs you both brought into the relationship.

Chances are, you entered your relationship hoping your partner would fulfill certain needs for you. For instance, perhaps you really wanted a family and felt he would be a good husband, father, and provider. Maybe you were happy to find someone who shared your religious beliefs, and felt that a like-minded base in faith was the most important "rock" upon which a couple must build a life together. Think about those needs now and indicate them in the table provided. Use the following inventory to identify the needs you had at the beginning of your relationship.

Physical Needs

_____ I, or my partner, was pregnant.

_____ I felt fulfilled by the intimacy we shared.

_____ I liked that my partner could take care of me.

_____ We liked the same activities and lifestyle.

_____ _____

Financial Needs

_____ I wanted the benefits of two incomes for a better lifestyle.

_____ I wanted the security of insurance and pension benefits.

_____ I wanted to travel and do things I couldn't afford on my own.

_____ I knew I could ease back on my job if I got married.

_____ I knew my partner could help me in my career.

_____ _____

Emotional Needs

_____ I was in love; I found my soulmate.

_____ I felt complete with my partner.

_____ I wanted a best friend, a companion.

_____ I was tired of dating around and we'd been going together for a while.

_____ All of my friends were married, and I wanted to be as well.

_____ I saw this as my last chance; I might not meet anyone else.

_____ I wanted to feel needed.

_____ I wanted the security of knowing someone was there for me.

_____ _____

Familial Needs

_____ I wanted children and a family of my own.

_____ I wanted to feel part of a family.

_____ I needed help taking care of my children from a previous marriage.

_____ I felt pressure from family and friends to get married.

_____ I liked the way my children and the person I was dating got along so well.

_____ _____

Intellectual Needs

_____   I wanted someone who would be mentally stimulating.

_____   I met someone with a similar educational background and the same interests.

_____   I found someone who encouraged me to help further my education.

_____   I wanted to learn from my partner's expertise/knowledge.

_____   _____

Spiritual Needs

_____   My partner shared my religious beliefs.

_____   My religious beliefs were that sex outside of marriage was wrong.

_____   My religious beliefs stressed the importance of marriage and family.

_____   _____

Other (If you had additional reasons, list them here. Be as specific as you can.)

_____   _____

_____   _____

_____   _____

What Needs Did Your Partner Bring to the Relationship?

Once you've completed this inventory, have your partner complete it also, if possible. If your partner is not available, complete the same inventory as if you were your spouse. Try to identify why your partner married you and what needs he or she expected you to satisfy. Think hard about this one; there may be reasons that you don't want to admit to yourself. Put yourself in your partner's shoes and try to see the relationship through his or her eyes. Focusing on your partner's needs can help you gain empathy for the expectations your partner brought to your marriage—expectations he or she relied on you to meet. And you'll see the ways in which our needs change over time, and why each person in the relationship must accept each person changing and adapt. You'll start to realize how such changes influence the relationship as a whole. In other words, one partner's changes can have an enormous impact not only on himself, but also on the other partner, and especially on the relationship itself.

How Well Did Your Relationship Meet Your Needs?

We're often disappointed when our partner fails to meet our needs. Sometimes, we're not even conscious of the needs we have. Other times, we fail to express them to our partner. We all expect our partners to be mind readers ("If he really loved me, he'd know what I want!"), but needs have to be specified. During the separation you've had the time to step back and look at yourself, to analyze who you are and what you want. Now is your opportunity to express your desires and listen to your partner express his.

When George and Marcy were able to sit down and talk, they found out that one of his important needs—feeling needed—hadn't been met by their old relationship. In fact, there hadn't even been an attempt to meet it because neither of them really knew that it existed, much less how important it was. For Marcy, she often felt suffocated in the old relationship. While George said he felt fine about her spending some time alone, he complained bitterly when she did. When it became clear how important their needs were to the life of the relationship, both partners agreed they could work together to fulfill them.

Marcy: "I knew that George resented my independence, and I resented that he did. But now that I have a better understanding of how much he enjoys feeling needed by me, I make sure he's aware that I really value his support."

George: "Marcy often told me she was hurt by my critical digs and that I didn't give her enough positive support. Now that I understand how strongly she needs appreciation for her accomplishments, I make a point of telling her how proud I am of her."

In order to have a successful reconciliation, you and your partner should find compromises that will allow needs to be met by each partner, to the extent possible. Each of us enters a relationship with our own special wishes and expectations that are very real even if they seem trivial or unimportant to our partner.

That Was Then...

In a satisfying marriage, there is a balance between needs and expectations. Each partner is aware of what is most important to the other and feels satisfied that their own important needs are being met. Problems start when there is a serious gap between our expectations and what we actually receive from the relationship.

Examine the needs you and your partner each had when you first entered the relationship. Be honest about how the relationship did or did not meet your individual needs. You were probably not quite as clear on your needs while you were going through the pain of slipping apart. There were too many hurtful emotions to think clearly. You might have felt the pain of unmet needs strongly but not have been able to articulate them. Now is your chance to be specific. Avoid vague generalities or accusatory statements, such as, "You never praised me." Instead, be as specific as you can—for example, "I really wanted you to congratulate me when I won the Employee of the Month award for working on the Baranko contract, and I was disappointed and hurt when you didn't." A generality doesn't tell your partner what you want; a specific example lets him know in terms he can act on. This conversation may take place over a course of days as you both delve deeper into the hopes and desires that first attracted you to each other. After examining the needs you had when you first started your relationship, you and your partner will be ready to discuss your current needs.

...This Is Now: What Needs Do You Have Now?

To determine your current needs, first look once more through the reasons why you came together. Look at the needs you checked. Were those needs met? Do you still have them? For some, the chief test is whether you still look to your partner to fill that need: Would you come together or get married today because of it? If the need is not strong enough to cause you to enter into a relationship again, consider it filled.

Next, think about your needs at this time—those that weren't present when you first met, but that have evolved throughout your marriage. The following list, with divisions into categories—physical, financial, emotional, familial, intellectual, and spiritual—will help you to inventory your current needs. Be specific. For example, under familial, you might put, "I need more time with my daughter." Take your time and come up with as complete a list as you can.

Examples of Basic Needs

Category	Needs
Physical	Food, shelter, clothing, sex, physical contact, exercise, safety, health care
Financial	Financial security, comfort items, basic expenses cared for, money for fun things, savings for future and retirement
Emotional	Love, commitment, emotional security, sharing, approval, understanding, recognition by peers, friendship, stability
Familial	Marriage/partnership, children, closeness to family, commitment to common goals, good parental relationship, time with spouse and children
Intellectual	Educational opportunity, mental stimulation, lively discussion, cultural activities (art/literature/music)
Spiritual	Spiritual belief, peace with self, concept of soulmate, integrity, time for solitude, closeness to nature/outdoors

Now think about how well each of your current needs is being filled. Go back to your list and, next to each need, write down whether it is filled or not and to what extent. You may find it helpful to "rate" each need by the percent it is filled. For example, now that you are earning a better income, your need for financial security may be 80 percent filled. Maybe your need for a best friend was 90 percent filled when you became close to someone at work or joined a social organization. Perhaps your need for approval was 70 percent filled when you were given a promotion at work or were elected to a leadership role in an organization. What role does your partner play in filling these needs? Give yourself time to consider where you are now in your relationship and how you feel about your needs now.

Also, go back to Chapter 4 and review the values you listed as important to you so that you are aware, when you and your partner begin speaking about reconciling, of how well they're reflected in the needs you have met.

Are Your Needs Compatible?

In discussing your current needs with your partner, it's important to consider which of your and your partner's needs are compatible and which are potential sources of conflict. For example, do you need more independence, while your spouse needs someone who always relies on her? Compromise and adjustment are necessary in any relationship. But if your needs and those of your partner are fundamentally different, it will be difficult for either of you to get what you want without causing serious discomfort to the other (unless you are able to find creative solutions). Again, talk about these differences to see if you can resolve your differing needs. Is it possible, or not? Suppose you married to gain a companion for fun activities, yet your spouse has a job that demands most of his time. During the week, he works late and on weekends he catches up on work he's brought home. You feel neglected, bored, and resentful. Obviously, the need for fun is unfilled. If this is still important to you, can you live without it? Are you willing to try new approaches?

How can you get this need met without including your partner, yet without putting a strain on the relationship?

These are not simple questions. Finding solutions and working out compromises requires thought. How important is a certain need to you? Will not having it filled create a serious dissatisfaction in your life? Was that need a primary reason you entered the relationship in the first place? Imagine that you met someone new today who is everything you want except for fulfilling that one particular need. Would you pursue the relationship?

No one can answer these questions but you (although a therapist can help you clarify your priorities). If things are not going to change, are you able to accept that and continue in this relationship? Are there other ways you can fill your needs? Keep in mind that the same questions apply to your partner as well. Will she be willing to accept unfilled needs? How important are they to her? If he sees that you will never be the one to help him fill them, will he stay with you or find other ways to get them met?

Everyone has needs that are valid and important. During the relationship our needs may be fulfilled completely, partially, or sometimes not at all. What's important right now is that you each identify your needs and discover ways to satisfy them. Again, the values you listed in Chapter 4 can serve as a guideline for both of you to identify what you really need for your happiness. If you and your partner are not yet talking to one another, go through these steps for yourself, and as with direction on previous exercises, complete your spouses as you think he or she would have filled it out. Once you do reconcile, be sure to "redo" this exercise together.

How Have You Both Changed?

Now that you and your partner have examined the needs you have in your relationship, turn your attention to the "new" people you have become. In what ways are your new selves compatible? You've both been through a lot, and have grown and changed tremendously. If you have used your separation time constructively, you will have developed more self-respect and self-confidence. You may also have changed in external ways. You may have gotten a new job, made new friends, taken up a hobby, or embarked on a fitness program. Let your partner know that you are not the same person you used to be, and ask him to share with you what changes he has experienced. Also discuss how these alterations have affected each of you. The following are some questions to help you and your partner get started talking about the changes. These can also be used as "stepping stones" to talk about the deeper, more emotional issues, making reconciling more feasible.

1. How have my daily habits changed? Have I changed my sleep hours, meal times, or other routine activities?

2. What new activities have I begun? Do I have new sports, hobbies, clubs? Have I begun taking classes?

3. What's going on at work? Have I gotten a promotion, a new project, new coworkers?

4. What's happened in my relationship with the children? What are we doing that we didn't do before? Am I seeing more of them or less? Am I treating them differently? What are my children's needs at this time? How has the separation affected them? What is their relationship with the absent partner?

5. How has my social life changed? Have I made new friends? Am I spending more/less time with old friends? What am I doing for fun these days?

6. What strengths and weaknesses have I discovered since the separation? What most surprised me about myself—something I never thought I could do, but did? In what areas do I wish I could be stronger?

7. What fears did I have during the separation? How did I handle them? What did I learn from them?

8. How do I feel about myself since the separation? How did my self-concept change during the months we were apart? Was there any one time when I felt myself changing? How?

9. What do I realize about my partner that I didn't realize before? How did my time apart make me understand him more? In what ways have my feelings toward him changed?

10. What do I realize about the relationship that I didn't realize before? How did the separation force me to view it in a new light? What did I learn?

11. If I were starting my marriage all over again, what would I do differently?

12. What did I most want to tell my partner on those long nights we were apart?

13. Have my partner and I been talking to each other openly and honestly? Do we treat each other with respect? Has communication improved? Are we able to talk about our needs, fears, past hurts, future dreams?

14. Have we both grown in awareness? Do we have better insights about what went wrong before and ways to avoid that in the future?

15. Do we avoid blaming each other? Have we learned to listen with our hearts as well as our ears?

16. Are we building trust and intimacy? Do we have a new history of interactions that support the relationship?

17. Are we having fun together? Do we enjoy each other's company? Can we laugh together?

18. Could we be friends? Do my partner and I genuinely like each other as people? Are we companions as well as lovers?

How Will These Changes Affect Your Relationship?

Examine with your partner how your new relationship will handle the changes that have taken place. For example, if you have gotten a new job that demands more of your time, how will that affect the relationship? If a promotion has made more money available, how will you spend it? If your partner has started spending more time with children from a previous marriage, how can that time be incorporated in your new relationship? Exploring the ways in which the relationship will be different, and how you will handle the changes, is another step in helping you decide whether the time is right to reconcile.

Be aware of old issues that might creep back into the relationship. Now that you have an opportunity to rebuild your relationship to be the way you wanted it all along, discuss any unfinished issues with your partner. George and Marcy's experiences during their separation helped them to clarify what they really wanted from a new relationship.

Marcy: "When George and I separated, I concentrated on my work, and spent the rest of my time thinking about what went wrong in our relationship, and writing for hours in a journal and analyzing my feelings. I understand myself much more now. I feel better than ever, and I'm a lot more confident in my abilities."

George: "I did just the opposite. When Marcy left me, I went crazy. I acted like a kid. I spent money like mad on a new car, new stereo system, new clothes. I did anything that would take my mind off what was happening. I even tried to get into another relationship, but I just couldn't make a go of it. My change took a lot longer than Marcy's. But when I finally took a closer look at myself and my needs, I realized that I wanted a more fulfilling, loving relationship—and that I wanted it with Marcy."

Although Marcy and George had completely different experiences during their separation, they both ended up learning a great deal about themselves and growing. When they got together to talk, they were surprised and pleased at the changes the other had gone through. Marcy was pleased to see that George had made new friends and no longer relied on her for companionship. George realized that he was proud of Marcy's new accomplishments and the way people praised how good she was at her job. When you and your partner discuss the changes that have occurred, you may be pleasantly surprised at the new things your partner can bring to the relationship.

Caution! Wait until You Can Both Commit to the Relationship

George and Marcy were both ready to give their best to a new relationship together. Both had worked on their own personal growth, identified their needs, and improved their communication with each other. Sometimes, though, one partner may not be as ready for reconciliation at the same time as the other. If either of you feels pushed or coerced into reconciliation, the chances of working it out this time are poor. There will be resentment, anger, and the feeling that one person has manipulated the other into a choice that wasn't mutual. The same problems that separated you in the first place will arise again.

There's always the possibility that the ambivalent person will not give the needed effort to make the relationship succeed. He may even make sure that it doesn't. When Susan learned that her husband, David, had stopped seeing the woman with whom he had been having an affair, she pleaded for him to move back home. "See, I told you it wouldn't work," David said, six weeks after they reconciled. Yielding to pressure, David had come home, but without a real commitment to create a good relationship with his wife. In fact, he even had yet to confront the demise of his failed relationship with his lover.

Can We Be a Couple Again?

Hopefully, unlike Susan and David, you and your partner have analyzed both your needs, and how they were and were not met by your relationship. Together, you've considered how you both have changed, and how that would affect a renewed relationship.

During the time you've been apart, you've had an opportunity to find your own identity and see your relationship from a new perspective. You've realized that you can find ways to fulfill your needs without relying on your partner to do so. You've talked with others, read, and gained insights about causes of the problems and possible solutions. If you've been using this book as a guide, you have probably already started to institute changes. Perhaps you've started an exercise program to release some of your stress; maybe you've gone back to school, or enrolled in a class to develop a long-standing interest. You may have started to build a new circle of friends whose interests more closely reflect yours. Perhaps you've become more involved in your work as a way of distracting yourself from pain about the relationship, or you may have started in counseling with a therapist. Continue doing these things when you reconcile. They are the things that have made you strong and given you a sense of self. They will continue to be valuable to you when you and your partner reconcile.

In discussing these changes with each other, remember the things you love in your partner that made all this work worthwhile. Remind each other of the good times and shared dreams:

how you first met, the first time you said "I love you," your joy when your children were born, the look on the grandparents' faces when they held the baby for the first time, the little things that demonstrated love, the shared secrets that made you meet each other's eyes and smile. Tell your partner what you respect and admire about her; what accomplishments you boast about to your friends; remind each other of shared accomplishments. Recognize the parts of your life that work well together. There is a lot of shared history between you that is joyous. Find the bonds between you and cherish them.

Questions for Reflection

1. What needs did I want my partner to fill when we first married?

    _____

    _____

2. If my partner did not fulfill the needs written above, have I found ways during our separation to have them met without relying on my partner (or did the needs resolve themselves on their own)?

    _____

    _____

3. What needs do I require from a partner now?

    _____

    _____

4. Can my partner fulfill my current needs, or have I found another way to fulfill them?

    _____

    _____

5. What differences do my partner and I still have? Do these need to be resolved before we reconcile or are they differences we can live with?

    _____

    _____

chapter _eight_

Communication: What Works and Why

Communication is the essence of a relationship because communication is how we connect with others and express our thoughts, feelings, hopes, fears, dreams, and expectations. Everything we do is a form of communication—our facial expressions, our body stance, our tone of voice, and all the other ways that we present ourselves and interact with others. When we communicate with a partner, we share ourselves, hoping that we'll be listened to, accepted, and understood. When communication breaks down, we feel that something important is missing, something that is vital to the lifeblood of the relationship.

No one has to tell you how important communication is to a relationship. Of all the factors that make for a successful relationship, communication is one of the most crucial. In good marriages, communication is the tie that binds couples strongly together. In relationships that need mending, lack of communication is one of the first signs of trouble. One of the primary problems you are no doubt facing right now is how to open the lines of communication in order to mend and build your relationship.

The ability to express yourself clearly, sharing what makes you feel loved, and setting limits for what you find to be tolerable or not, are essential in any relationship. These are doubly important for couples trying to reconcile their differences and get back together.

Being able to communicate effectively can help you work toward dissolving the conflicts that kept you apart while opening up new possibilities for being together. It can help rebuild trust and hope in areas you thought were irreparably destroyed. Good communication can take you to deeper levels of sharing and intimacy than you ever thought possible.

How many times have you said about your partner, "She doesn't understand me"? Or, "He just doesn't 'get it'"? In relationships that need mending, the wrong kinds of communication (silence, threatening, yelling, recriminations) are usually the first signs of trouble. When your best efforts to reach understanding are continually frustrated, it can make you feel as if there is little hope. What you need now are new skills for opening the lines of communication so that healing and rebuilding your relationship are possible.

Speaking from Your Heart

Talking comes naturally; communicating well is a skill that can be learned. Although you've acquired proven tools for communicating more effectively, you may still have questions about how to deal with specific issues and circumstances. Even if you are not able to dialogue with your partner at this time, practice with your family and friends so that you will be prepared when the opportunity arises.

The main principle to remember is that the more honestly and openly you speak, the more simply and clearly you reveal what is in your heart, the more likely it is that you will open deeper channels of communication.

When you speak from the heart, there is no pretense, no blaming, no covering up. If you are simply stating what is true for you and listening for understanding, it is likely that you will trigger an equally honest response. Even if your partner is not able to communicate completely openly at this time, you are establishing a foundation for the future.

Communication and Soulmates

If you've experienced those precious moments when you and your partner were totally tuned in to each other, when you were both on the same wavelength, sharing the same thoughts and feelings, then you know what people mean when they refer to their partner as their soulmate. You each opened your heart to the other.

> "So many times," Christopher said of his relationship to Diane, "we don't even have to say a word. It's like I know what she's thinking, or she knows what I'm thinking. Here's a good example: The other night we were watching a movie, but my mind kept going back to my ill father. Diane turned to me and said, 'You're thinking about your dad, aren't you? Perhaps you should fly back to see him.' That kind of thing happens to us all the time. That she knows me so well makes me love her so much."

Christopher and Diane have achieved the kind of understanding and closeness that creates an enduring bond. Why is it so hard for many well-intentioned women and men to reach this level of closeness? Let's take a look at some of the main obstacles.

What You Said Versus What You Meant: Obstacles to Communication

How often have you carefully worded a statement, only to say, "Oh, that came out all wrong. What I really meant to say was . . ."? Perhaps you think you heard your partner say one thing, only to find out she said something else. Or you showed up for an appointment and found that you misunderstood the time or the day it was scheduled? Somewhere between what was said and what you heard, the meaning got altered.

Maybe you find yourself disagreeing on the meanings of words. A friend says, "What a beautiful blue," and you answer, "That's not blue, that's green." Or your partner says, "Let's go someplace different for vacation this year," and you think, "Oh good, I've been wanting to visit that new luxury resort." But he was imagining roughing it on a whitewater rafting trip. Blue, green, different, same, spicy, bland, hot, cold—all mean different things to different people.

Since we're all unique individuals, with our own unique backgrounds, expectations, and beliefs, we all experience and interpret words and events differently—which leads us to react differently. You might believe that if you communicate well, your partner will agree with what you're saying. But communication involves much more than speaking—it also involves listening, really listening. Empathic listening means that we listen not only to the words, but also to the feelings and intentions beneath them. We allow our partner to express himself, and try to place ourselves in his position in order to understand his point of view. We accept this view as valid for him, even though we may not agree with it. In other words, knowing how to listen is just as important as, or even more important than, knowing how to talk.

How to Talk So Your Partner Will Listen— And Listen So Your Partner Will Talk

Studies have shown several key factors that govern how we experience our environment and perceive others. One of these factors is our individual style of processing incoming information—our perceptual mode, which literally determines how we experience people and the world around us.

The three basic perceptual modes are visual, auditory, and kinesthetic. Most people are visual—they "see" what you mean—and how they see things governs how they feel about them. Others are auditory—things "sound good" to them, or else they "don't like the sound of that." The third group of people are kinesthetic perceivers—they "have a feel for things" or they go by their "gut reactions."

Visual and kinesthetic people tend to be governed more by their emotions. Auditory folks are usually more analytical and linear in their approach. Although there are always exceptions, understanding these differences is vital. Misunderstandings are most likely to occur when two people have different predominant modes of processing information—for example, when a person who is predominantly auditory gives verbal instructions to a person who is predominantly visual.

"Do You See What I Mean?"
Visual people tend to forget what has been said very quickly. Out of sight is literally out of mind—words seem to disappear into thin air. So if you're exasperated with your partner because you keep asking him to do something and he hasn't, or he never remembers to stop and bring home what you called him about at the office, try writing notes and leaving them where he'll be sure to see them— like the dashboard of the car or the door you want him to fix.

"Tell Me That You Love Me"
Auditory people think in words, rather than images or feelings. They have to hear themselves talk in order to know what they think. They need lengthy discussions in order to come to a decision. They describe things in great detail and ask many questions. They like to keep in frequent verbal contact, and they will remember what you said. To get your point across, be prepared for lengthy conversations with your verbal partner!

"I Know How You Feel"
A kinesthetic person would rather hold your hand and commune silently than tell you verbally how much you mean to him. It's not that he doesn't care—it's that words don't mean as much to him as the reassuring pressure of a hand. He's more apt to wash your car as a way of communicating love. For the kinesthetic person, actions speak louder than words. But if you're verbal, you need to hear the words, "I love you." Hold his hand or hug him as you tell him that you want to hear, "I love you." This way, he'll feel what you mean.

One of the most important things you can do to improve communication between you and your partner is to become aware of your own processing and communication style. Are you predominantly visual, auditory, or kinesthetic? The following checklist will help you determine your processing and communication style. Check the column that is true for you.

What Is Your Communication Style?	Yes	No
I need to see things to understand them.	____	____
I like to get the big picture.	____	____
I want people to see my point of view.	____	____
For me, seeing is believing.	____	____
Appearance is important to me.	____	____
I remember conversations.	____	____
I can talk and work at the same time.	____	____
I don't have to look at someone to talk to him.	____	____
I often talk to myself when I'm deciding something.	____	____
I like to tell all the details when I talk about something.	____	____
My feelings are easily hurt.	____	____
I go by my gut feelings.	____	____
It's easier for me to learn by doing.	____	____
I use my hands when I talk.	____	____
I can commune with someone I'm close to without talking.	____	____

If most of your "yes" answers were to the first five statements, you're primarily visual, and you perceive the world in a visual way. You would rather see a picture than hear something described. The saying "One picture is worth a thousand words" describes your way of looking at things. You want people to look at you while you're talking to them so that you can watch their reactions and feel that they're paying attention. You definitely don't want your partner to yell, "But I can hear you!" from the other room. It's probably easier for you to find your way to a strange place with a map, than by listening to directions. And if you don't have your shopping list, you might wonder, "Now what did I come here to buy?"

The next five statements in the previous inventory describe auditory people. If you're auditory, you have an excellent verbal memory—often remembering things almost word for word. You can tell your partner what he said last month or remember detailed instructions. You can easily be working at your computer while carrying on a conversation. Lots of internal chatter goes on in your head. You're usually comfortable talking in front of large groups and can "think on your feet" and field questions easily.

The last five statements of the inventory describe people who are kinesthetic. Do you become tearful in sad movies, use your hands when you talk, find your stomach tightening when someone else is tense, and learn better by actually doing than being told? If you have these traits, you are kinesthetic. Things "feel" either right or wrong to you. When things don't feel right, it disturbs you. You go with your hunches or gut reactions. You relate easily to other people's feelings and you especially want your partner to be aware of yours. You empathize readily—you can actually feel the other person's happiness or pain. People may accuse you of being oversensitive.

These are guidelines. No one is exclusively one perceptual mode or another, but most people have one preferred (or dominant) mode of accessing and processing information, and one or two secondary modes. Some people can use all three modes equally well, and because they can switch between modes easily, they're usually excellent communicators. They can always "talk the other person's language," whatever style that might be. But difficulties arise when partners start talking right past each other because they're not communicating in the language mode that the other prefers. For example, probably one of the most common arguments that arises between visual and auditory partners stems from the request, "Look at me when I'm talking to you." The auditory person answers, "I can hear you" (while reading the newspaper, or watching TV or even from another room!). What he doesn't realize is that a visual person needs her partner to look at her while she talks. She has to be able to see that he is paying attention and understands what she's saying. She wants to be able to watch him in order to "see" his reaction. Otherwise she feels that her partner just doesn't care, or hasn't heard.

To find out your partner's primary communication mode, go back to the "What Is Your Communication Style?" checklist that you filled out for yourself, and this time, ask your partner to fill it out. Now compare your inventories: Do you and your partner share the same communication style, or are you different in your approach? Discuss how your differences have affected the quality of your communication in the past. How can you accommodate your differences? While you are talking with your partner, observe how his predominant communication style is expressed. The next time you want to communicate something important, be sure to put it in his processing mode so that your message has maximum impact. For example, if you want to build more intimacy with your partner, you could say:

Visual: "I really enjoy seeing us do things together. It seems like we've become much closer."

Auditory: "When I listen to you talk about our future, I can hear how much closer we've become."

Kinesthetic: "It feels good, like we're really close when we spend time together."

As you become more skilled at talking in your partner's preferred language mode, you'll notice that communication improves. Keep in mind that unless you literally speak his language, he won't fully see, hear, or feel what you're trying to convey. Ideally, each of you will care enough to learn about the other's preferred style and, when you do, you'll have a better chance of really tuning in to each other.

Guidelines for Communicating Effectively

In addition to speaking to your partner in her language, there are a number of basic principles of good communication that have been time-tested and proven effective. If you familiarize yourself with them and practice using them until they become second nature, you'll find that communication between you and your partner improves.

Practice these communication skills regularly. As with anything new, at the beginning they may seem awkward and artificial, but give them a chance and use them. Eventually they'll come naturally. You may need to modify some of these techniques so they fit your own personal style and feel more natural. That's okay. Whatever you do, keep practicing! Remember, your goal is to reunite with your partner and to make your new relationship better than ever. One of the most important ways you'll do that is by communicating effectively with your partner in mind.

At this point, you may be separated, with very little or only hostile exchanges with your partner. Maybe you're communicating regularly, but still experiencing difficulties and frustrations in getting your point of view across. Or perhaps you've reached the point where you're actively discussing reconciliation. You may even have already reconciled and be looking for a way to make sure things work out this time. Whatever point you're at, communication is the most important key to reaching into the heart and soul of the relationship. So even if you're apart and not currently having a lot of contact with your partner, read these examples and learn them on your own so you can apply them in the future when you and your partner are ready to talk. (After we explain these techniques, we'll tell you what to do if your partner won't communicate.) These eight principles are proven tools for communicating more clearly with each other so that you can understand what each of you is really trying to say. When you and your partner understand each other better, you'll be on your way to a more meaningful and fulfilling relationship. So, let's get started!

1. Tell how you feel.

Use "I" statements, such as: "I want, I hope, I feel . . ." to let your partner know what the impact of her behavior is on you.

> EXAMPLE: "Even though we're separated, I want us to remain friends. When you make decisions about the children without consulting me, I feel that my wishes are unimportant to you." Or, when you move toward reconciliation: "When we talk honestly to each other, I feel really close to you. I want us to continue sharing our thoughts and feelings with each other. I hope you agree."

Your partner's desires and hopes may differ from yours, but you can clearly express your own without blaming. You can't expect your partner to change because you feel a certain way, but you can communicate your feelings clearly. No matter how long you've been together, your partner may not know how you feel about a situation. When you clearly state how you feel and what you want without blaming, you give him the opportunity to respond without feeling defensive. And when you share your hopes, you reveal more about the things that are important to you.

2. Ask for what you want.

Ask for what you want directly. Directness goes with "I" statements. Instead of saying, "You never call when you say you will" or "Why don't you ever take the children for an outing?"—both of which assign blame—state your wants directly.

> EXAMPLE: "I'd like us to start building trust so that I know I can count on you. If you want to join us for a picnic on Sunday, we'll be leaving here at 11:00."

3. Be brief.

Be concise when you talk, to avoid overloading your partner and having him tune out. An excellent exercise is to state your wants in twenty-five words or less.

> EXAMPLE: "I need your help on Saturday to take Bruce to Little League while I take Joni to the dentist."

Communicating like this not only shows respect, but it also gets better results than saying, "I'm fed up with your being so irresponsible. Why don't you ever think of us instead of just doing what's convenient for you?" By omitting blame and getting to the point, you reduce your partner's natural reaction to defend himself, and you create an opportunity for change.

4. Be specific.

Be specific instead of using vague words like "closeness" and "caring." Rather than saying something like, "You never show me you care," which is a blaming statement that really doesn't let your partner know what you want, translate your desires into specific behaviors that you would like at certain times. This is especially important as you begin to move toward reconciliation.

> EXAMPLE: "When we get together again, I'd like us to continue developing more closeness by sitting down together for twenty minutes when we get home from work and sharing what went on during the day."

This may seem somewhat artificial at first, but your partner may have often felt confused by demands for "more consideration," "more caring," or "more intimacy." Even though it may seem difficult at first, asking for what you want directly is a communication skill that both of you can learn to use effectively.

5. Watch what your body language and voice tone are saying.

Be aware of your nonverbal messages. Your body language, voice tone, and words must all match to send a clear message.

If your words say one thing, but your body posture or voice tone conveys something else, you're sending a mixed message. Your partner will feel either confused or resentful. She may decide that you really don't know what you want or will choose to respond to the message that's most convenient. For example, perhaps you have trouble expressing anger and therefore tend to cover up your feelings. When you try to express anger about a situation, you may smile nervously and speak hesitantly, so that you're not taken seriously.

If you feel discomfort when expressing yourself about a situation that you feel strongly about, rehearse first in front of a mirror. Practice taking deep breaths and using your whole body when you speak so that your tone will be deeper and more assertive. Make sure that your body stance and facial expression fit the message you want to convey.

EXAMPLE: Stand comfortably straight, with feet apart, look directly at your partner and say in a firm tone, "I feel disappointed and angry when you cancel our plans at the last minute. It makes me feel that you don't respect my time. I realize emergencies can come up, but I want you to keep your commitments with me."

6. Present alternatives.

Give your partner some alternatives. We're all more likely to respond positively to situations when we're given a choice and have some control over outcomes. Providing options helps set the stage for mutual problem solving.

> EXAMPLE: "There's a good movie playing. Let's get a babysitter and go see it Saturday night. But if your brother decides to come over, we could go Sunday instead."

7. Use active listening.

Let your partner know she has your full attention. Maintain eye contact and nod, or give verbal cues that show understanding or agreement. It also helps to restate in your own words what your partner has said to make sure you understand.

> EXAMPLE: "It sounds like you really want to get out and do something. Tell you what—if Andy comes over Saturday night, we'll go see the movie on Sunday for sure."

8. Show empathy.

Give your partner feedback in a way that shows you understand his position, even if you don't agree with it. Let him know your reaction in a way that doesn't require either of you to justify yourselves, but leaves the door open for negotiation and change.

> EXAMPLE: "I understand that it's important for your career to put in a lot of overtime, but I feel lonely and I miss you when you're not here."

What to Do If Your Partner Doesn't Want to Communicate

Despite your good communication skills, your partner may simply not want to talk to you. He cuts you off, leaves the room, changes the topic, or in some other way makes clear that whatever you wanted to discuss is a subject that he would prefer to ignore. Or, since you have separated, perhaps she won't return your calls, or is hostile when you do talk. While you want to put all your cards on the table, solve problems, and come to a resolution, your partner may insist that there is no problem, or that it's already been solved, or that he's tired of talking about it. In spite of your best efforts, it appears that the meaningful communication you want so badly is not going to take place. What should you do?

Trying to get a resistant partner to open up and start talking about issues of concern to you can be a frustrating goal. If the issue has been previously addressed, step back and identify just what emotional need you want fulfilled by your partner. Is it acknowledgment? Is it reassurance? Is it comfort? If the issue is emotionally laden, the tendency is to want to pursue it. However, rather than focus on the specific topic, express your underlying feelings. Go back to Step 1 and use "I" statements, letting your partner know clearly what you need.

> EXAMPLE: Instead of saying something like, "Are you sure you don't want to see Gloria anymore?" say something like, "Despite the fact that everything has been great since we've been back together, I still keep getting flashes of you together with Gloria. It makes me feel very anxious—I need to hear you say that I'm the only one in your life."

There may be other times when you want to explore issues that your partner is uncomfortable with. If he avoids discussion, you may become angry and doubt that he's really committed to the relationship. "Why doesn't he want to work this out?" you ask. There are a number of reasons that he may be avoiding communication. Here are some common reasons and what you can do about them.

The Issue Has Already Been Dealt With

This may be an issue that has been talked out with your partner and resolved, but that continues to haunt you. Your need to reopen it may really be a desire for reassurance. When Rita and Paul reconciled, Paul broke off with the girlfriend he had been seeing during the separation. He told Rita that he wanted to be married to her more than anything else in the world. All his actions bore out his commitment to their relationship.

But Rita was unsure. Was Paul still harboring romantic feelings about his former girlfriend? Did he think she was sexier or more attractive than Rita? Rita wanted to be reassured. Specifically, she wanted to hear Paul say that he was sorry about what he had done, that Rita was still the love of his life, and that he would never stray again.

> What You Can Do: It would have been better, when Rita became aware of her need for reassurance, if she had asked for it directly. She could have told Paul, "I love you and trust you, but I need reassurance. I need to hear that I'm the person who's most desirable to you."

The Issue Feels Too Painful to Discuss

Your partner may be feeling shame or guilt about past actions. Such feelings are very painful, and he may be trying to deal with them by denying them. It can be easier to say, "It never happened" about a situation he now regrets than to talk about it and try to explain why it happened. As a general rule, the more guilt your partner feels, the more likely she is to deny the situation, try to minimize it, or just refuse to discuss it.

What You Can Do: Recognize that the most important thing is for your partner to confront these painful feelings. Rather than focus on the details of the event, help him to express his feelings about it. "I know it must be very painful for you when you think about how your seeing Gloria affected the level of trust in our marriage. I just want you to know I realize how hard it is to talk about, and I'm willing to just listen any time you're ready."

Your Partner Has a Need for Privacy

Persistent questioning can feel intrusive. Although communication is the heart of a good relationship, demands such as "tell me what you're thinking" can feel like an invasion of privacy. Your partner may need to keep a certain amount of information about his activities (however trivial they may be) to himself. This is not out of a desire to keep secrets, but rather a need to feel that he is able to maintain personal space, in which certain areas of his life belong to him alone.

What You Can Do: Remind yourself that your partner may need more psychological space than you do. Tell yourself, "It's not really important; if it were, he'd tell me. Right now, however minor it may seem, he needs it to be his secret." We all harbor some thoughts that we do not wish to disclose to our partner.

Your Communication Styles Differ

Some processing and communication styles don't lend themselves to a great deal of verbal self-examination. Especially for kinesthetic and visual individuals, "putting something away" is literally that. They have filed the past away and are able to retrieve it only by resurrecting the original painful memories and re-experiencing them. Naturally, they are reluctant to do so. One year after Tom and Paula's reconciliation, Tom has still not divulged certain activities that he engaged in during their separation. He insists, "It's over. It belongs in the past."

> What You Can Do: If this is your situation, it helps to remind yourself that there are some things you may never know, but that your partner loves you, and the things you don't know are probably irrelevant to your new relationship. Seek your reassurance from her actions, words, and positive attitudes toward your relationship in the present.

Communication Skills That Build Love

Fear of how your partner will react is one of the primary barriers to good communication. In such situations, a structured approach can help by allowing each of you to express yourselves in a way that leads to acceptance and understanding, instead of defensiveness or blame. It is also a way to get through communication barriers to a level of openness where you can discuss important issues.

> "When things started to go wrong with my company," says Mark, " I felt like such a failure; I couldn't face telling my wife, Colleen. Instead, I confided in a woman friend and ended up having an affair. It was the stupidest things I've ever done! When Colleen finally found out, she was furious and told me to leave.
>
> "It was a really hard time for me. I always resisted counseling, but I finally admitted that I needed help and started seeing a therapist. After a few agonizing months of separation, Colleen eventually agreed to see me, and we gradually started to really communicate.

"One of the things that helped most was having a structure for our communication. It kept us on track when we talked, instead of going off on tangents. Also, it made it easier to talk about difficult issues. I tend to hold things in and avoid addressing problems. Colleen wants to explore and get to the bottom of issues. I was feeling so guilty about what I put her through all those months I was cheating on her that I was afraid I might not be totally honest. But I also knew that there was no chance of any reconciliation with Colleen unless I was willing to be completely open with her.

"This framework for talking helped. When we finally were able to tell each other what was really going on inside, it was a huge relief—and the beginning of our getting back together."

Saying What You Mean and Hearing What Is Said

Structuring your communication might seem unnatural at first, but you will find that it is a powerful communication tool that helps you express your feelings and needs more easily and openly.

To begin, agree on a time and place where you can be together and undisturbed for at least one hour. Read the first question (Dialogue 1, next page), and then take three minutes to write down your answer. (Writing is often easier for those who have more difficulty with verbal expression.) Write your thoughts down quickly, without worrying about spelling or grammar. Just let the words pour out. Set a timer so you do not go past three minutes.

When the three minutes are up, stop writing and take turns reading your answers to each other. Maintain eye contact and listen with the intent of fully understanding your partner. Do not interrupt or think about what you are going to say while your partner is reading. Above all, be sure to listen with your heart, as well as your ears, so you are aware of the feelings behind the words you're hearing.

After each of you has read your answers, sit quietly for a moment and reflect on what you have heard. Then take two minutes each to respond, acknowledging what your partner said, before moving on to the next dialogue.

Dialogue 1: What I Value about You

EXAMPLE: Mark was the first to read. "What I value most about you, Colleen, is your warm heart and loving spirit. I love the way you laugh so easily and find fun in so many different things. You've really opened my eyes to the fact that life doesn't always have to be so serious. I value your honesty. I know that the answers you give me are the truth. Even though I don't always like what I hear, I'm really glad that you always level with me. Last, but not least, I love how good you make me feel!"

Colleen's eyes brightened as she listened to Mark, then it was her turn. "Mark, I value how you've been such a support in my life. You're not the most talkative person, but when you say something, I know it comes from the heart. I value how you're able to admit mistakes and are willing to work so hard to make things right. I know that going into counseling was a big step for you. I really appreciate your working so hard on our relationship. You're like my rock—I know you're always looking out for me."

Mark and Colleen were pleasantly surprised that they each found so many things they valued in the other. Colleen was especially delighted that Mark valued her love of fun and her playfulness. It pleased her to discover that what she thought might be a weakness was really a source of joy to Mark. Mark didn't realize that what he thought of as a too-serious demeanor was really valued by Colleen, who appreciated him for being a solid presence that she could rely on. It gave him a sense of pride to know that the dependability he thought might be too boring for Colleen was instead something she valued.

Dialogue 2: What I Need to Feel Secure

EXAMPLE: Colleen: "Mark, what I need from you to feel secure is to know that I'm the only woman in your life. I want to be number one in your heart and know that I'm not only your wife, but also your best friend, lover, and confidante. I need you to always tell me the truth, and talk to me the next time you run into problems so we can handle them together. Most important, I want to feel that you are totally committed to our relationship and will keep working on making it strong."

Mark: "I need to know that you are glad to be my wife, that you believe in our marriage, and are willing to hang in there with me as we work things out. I need reassurance that you accept me despite my flaws, and that you don't regret choosing me as your husband. I'm better at doing than talking, so it would mean a lot to me to feel that you notice the little things I do to show my love for you. Most important, I need to know that you still love me."

Trust and fidelity are the two most important areas where partners need to feel secure. When a relationship is in trouble, addressing these issues is even more critical. We have to believe that no one else can take our place, and that there is a bond of mutual trust and honest communication.

Dialogue 3: What I Need from This Relationship

EXAMPLE: Mark: "I want a relationship that makes us happy and is strong enough to withstand anything that comes along. I need our relationship to be my sanctuary, where I can kick back and relax with you, talk about anything that's on my mind, and know that no matter what happens, I have a best friend. I always want to look forward to coming home with the feeling, 'I can't wait to be with Colleen!'"

Colleen: "What I need from this relationship is for it to be very loving, solid, and committed. I want our marriage to be the most important thing in our lives. I also want it to be a very fun, comfortable relationship, where we can laugh and be silly like a couple of kids. Especially, I want our relationship to be a haven where we both feel completely protected and loved."

Every relationship really contains three entities: you, your partner, and the relationship. In making decisions, you have to decide not only how it will affect you and your partner, but also how it will affect your relationship. Making it strong and healthy so that it can withstand inevitable ups and downs is your most important job.

Dialogue 4: These Are My Concerns

EXAMPLE: Colleen: "My biggest concern is that you might get stressed out again, and despite the progress we've made, you would have another affair. I need a lot of reassurance because I don't ever want to start suspecting you again. I worry that once we get back together, we might start slipping into old habits, and not share our feelings as openly as we do now—that maybe you would shut down again, and not tell me what's going on."

Mark: "I'm concerned that I might start getting too focused on business again, and not take the time to do all the things I know are needed to keep our marriage strong. Without even meaning to, I could start neglecting what really is important. It's been a long, hard road to rebuild the trust between us, and I'm concerned that you might give up on me. I love you, and I care very much about making it up to you for the hurt I've caused.

I might never succeed completely, but I'll do everything in my power to make sure our marriage is the best it can be!"

Concerns and anxieties rooted in painful experiences take time to diminish and then fade away. When you first get back together, there is always a residue of unease. This is completely natural—the more you have been hurt, the longer it takes to forget. Even though you decide to forgive and move on with a clean slate, emotional scars heal at their own pace. A word, a gesture, or a late phone call can all trigger memories you would rather forget. Keep reminding yourself that you are building a bond of trust between you, and use the communication skills that you have acquired. In time, as you strengthen your relationship, these doubts will slowly fade away and cease to exist.

Dialogue 5: My Hopes for Our Relationship

EXAMPLE: Colleen: "My biggest hope for the relationship is that we can continue to communicate and grow together, the way we have in the last few months. I want us to keep sharing what's going on, and take care of any problems that come up right away. I've learned so much about you—it's made it a lot easier for me to understand what happened, and what we need to do in the future. I also want us to get counseling whenever we feel stuck. In the next few years, I also want us to start a family."

Mark: "I hope that we will continue building the love and trust between us. We've gotten through some very rough spots, and I just want our marriage to keep getting stronger. I want to start building up a nest egg for our future family. But before we have children, I want us to go to Europe. That's been a big dream of mine!"

When Colleen and Mark started this dialogue process, they were unaccustomed to revealing their feelings so openly. But they quickly discovered that the structure made it easier to express their true feelings. The experience was so positive they decided to allot a regular time for it each week.

"I don't every think we'll ever forget how important it is to communicate," Mark said. "But if we hit any rough spots, we can use what we've learned to talk about them." Colleen nodded in agreement, "I really enjoy how we've opened up to each other. I've learned so much about you, Mark. I only knew the tip of the iceberg before—now I'm really convinced we have something special."

Questions for Reflection

1. Am I primarily a visual, auditory, or kinesthetic communicator? What is my partner?

   _____

   _____

2. If my partner and I have different styles of communication, how can we accommodate our differences?

   _____

   _____

3. What things do I most want to say to my partner?

   _____

   _____

4. How will I tell my partner what I need without blaming him/her for not providing it in the past?

   _____

   _____

5. Why do I think my partner sometimes refuses to communicate, and what can I do about it?

   _____

   _____

chapter *nine*

Now That You're Back Together:
How to Avoid the Pitfalls of Reconciliation

You've come a long way since you first separated and decided to seek reconciliation. Your commitment to a constructive plan of action to love your way back into the relationship succeeded, and now you and your partner are back together—learning to be with each other in new ways.

Yet, despite the excitement of being reunited, somewhere in the back of your mind there's a small voice that keeps whispering things like, "Are you positive you should trust this? What if he leaves again? What if I have to go through all that chaos and pain again? What makes you think that this is going to last?" Lingering doubts can make you feel insecure even at the best of times. Right now, when you're most vulnerable, even though you try to ignore them, those nagging doubts probably won't go away.

These feelings are a natural part of the coming-together process. You have high hopes for the new relationship, and neither of you may be able to entirely fulfill those hopes at this time. Or, you may anticipate an unrealistic degree of change on the part of your partner, forgetting that growth is a continuous process.

You may also demand too much of yourself. You are justifiably proud of the progress you have made, and you feel much more confident in your ability to handle the relationship. Don't expect to suddenly be able to manage all the circumstances that come along. Have your expectations, dream your dreams, but root them in reality, and remember that progress occurs one small step at a time.

Common Stumbling Blocks in Reconciliation

What can you expect, now that you are back together? You know that everything won't be perfect; there will be up days and down days. How can you deal with the days when things seem to be falling apart? Here is an overview of some of the most common problems newly reconciled couples encounter and suggestions for handling them.

You Feel There Are Still Unanswered Questions

Frances and Paul had been married for what Frances called "four of the happiest years of my life." Then Paul began to have business problems that caused him to become sullen and withdrawn. Things got so bad that their marriage became, in Frances' words, "a nightmare," which led to separation.

After several months, during which they kept in touch, Paul abruptly did a complete reversal. He left his former business, dropped some acquaintances that had caused him trouble, and changed back to his former loving and affectionate self. One afternoon he appeared at Frances' door and told her he was ready to "pick up where we left off—and I don't want to talk about what happened!"

Frances was thrilled to have Paul back. However, she became intensely frustrated when he refused to discuss the reasons for his previous actions toward her. As far as he was concerned, the past was over, and he wanted to leave it there. "I'm back; let's leave it at that," he'd say. The more Frances tried to talk about their former problems, the more Paul became irritable and withdrawn. Finally, afraid of losing him again, Frances let the matter drop. But it made her really uncomfortable that he wouldn't talk about an issue that had been so devastating to their marriage.

While you were apart, you talked about your relationship to your friends, your family, your therapist, and just about anyone who would listen. You couldn't wait to get back together with your partner and discuss things. Many times you said, "If only we could sit down and really communicate, everything would be so much better." During the reconciliation process, the two of you did open up and have those heart-to-heart talks about important issues, and you both gained greater understanding.

But now that you are together again, things may be different. There may still be unanswered questions or issues you want to discuss, but your partner does not. During the separation, your partner may have been more willing to speak openly to resolve the problems and get back together. Now that you are reunited, your partner may feel that there is no more need to talk. After all, he reasons, why bring up the past and all its pain all over again?

This may be really frustrating for you. On the surface, it's difficult to argue with, "Let's move on and focus on our lives now; let's not keep talking about the past." It all sounds so rational. Yet, the issues that concern you may still feel unresolved. There's no one magical moment in which your heart says, "Okay, that's it. We've now talked about the crisis long enough, and I am officially healed." Everyone heals at a different pace. Your spouse may be perfectly content with the new state of affairs and not need further discussion. You, on the other hand, may still be looking for explanations, so that you can understand what happened and move on.

Your partner may be frustrated, as well; she honestly feels that everything that needs to be said has been said. She can't understand why you want to keep going over and over the same painful events. Your partner may even begin to resent your continuing efforts to talk about the past when she wants to focus on the present. In Chapter 8 we explained how different processing styles can interfere with communication and gave reasons why your partner may not feel the need to express himself as fully as you do. If he has difficulty exploring a particular issue, use empathic communication to make open dialog in this area more possible. If your partner still says "no," then you have to decide if it's an area you're willing to let "slide" or something you need to do something about as soon as possible. This is another reason you should consider seeing a therapist to help you gain perspective, or find an outlet in a support group, which provides an opportunity to share your experiences and learn from others about how others handled similar issues.

You're Afraid of Causing Arguments

A second common problem during reconciliation is the fear of causing arguments. Everything is going so well now, you reason. Your partner is back, you're in love again; things should be perfect. So when he does something that upsets you, you rationalize it and find excuses, or you harbor it and resent him without sharing the fact that you're upset. After all, the last thing you want to do is start another argument. You may be afraid that even the smallest argument might escalate into a major upheaval that would result in his leaving again.

Yet you can't just gloss over problems. Perhaps doing that is what led to the deterioration of your relationship in the first place. If you let the small irritations grow into larger ones, you eventually explode—or you hold the feelings inside you and let your resentment out in indirect ways that undermine the relationship. Unexpressed concerns start a dangerous cycle in which you hold your partner responsible for things that she doesn't even know are bothering you.

One source of conflict between Frances and Paul before their separation was continuous fights over how little time Paul spent with the family. Paul felt he was giving as much of himself as he could and that it was unreasonable to expect more. A few months after they reunited, Frances again asked Paul to spend more time at home. When Paul showed signs of annoyance ("You're not going to start that up again, are you, just when things are going so well?") Frances backed off immediately. She had no intention of causing a blow-up at this stage.

Yet she knew that she had compromised her principles. Frances felt strongly that Paul should spend more time with his family and started to question just how committed Paul truly was. Because she had allowed him to cut off a discussion due to her fear that it would turn into a fight, a very important matter went unresolved.

What Frances could have done was let Paul know that even though he wasn't prepared to discuss it with her at that time, the matter was critical to her and something they needed to resolve at a time they both agreed on.

You're Not Ready to Fully Trust the New Relationship

"For the first few months after Paul came back, I didn't withdraw my petition for divorce. I didn't go forward with it either. I thought that since Paul had changed so much in the six months before the separation, I had no way of knowing that he wouldn't change again. It seemed as if everything had happened overnight, as if I went to bed with my husband and woke up with a stranger. I was afraid that Paul might shift that quickly again.

"As much as I loved Paul, I had to face the reality of the situation. Sure, Paul came back, but he could leave again at any time. This nervousness ruled me for several months. It wasn't until we had been together again for about three months that I got comfortable enough, secure enough, to drop the divorce suit. Luckily for me, Paul was willing to wait. He told me we were back together for life, and the separation was just a bad memory. I think it was his utter certainty about the permanence of our relationship, more than anything else, that finally convinced me."

Once burned, twice shy. Even though you love your partner and have been longing for the time you would be back together with her, deep down inside of you there may be something holding you back—something that keeps you from giving your all. You just don't think you could go through all that pain again, or survive "redoing" your life, and you're terrified of putting yourself in a position to go through all that again.

Wanting to succeed, yet also wanting to protect yourself, creates a real bind. On the one hand, it's natural to be afraid of something that has the potential to hurt you deeply. On the other, you have to commit to the relationship totally in order to make it work. Not committing allows you to say, "I knew it wouldn't work out; I was right to hold something back," but it also sabotages the very thing you want most: a fresh new beginning.

Remember that your partner is also feeling insecure right now. He probably feels the same anxiety that you do—or even more. If he is the one who left, he may be thinking, "It's her turn now; when is she going to leave me?" Or, your partner may feel that since she hurt you so badly, it's only a matter of time until you decide to get even. The key is not to let negative feelings and fears overwhelm you and the new love you have.

You're Not Yet Able to Trust Again

"When Paul and I were apart, he went out with his former girlfriend, a woman he had dated before we were married. I couldn't stop thinking of the two of them laughing, having sex, maybe discussing our marriage. How can I make love with Paul again, knowing he cheated on me? My rational mind tells me that it wasn't cheating, that we were separated, and that I was the one who had filed for divorce. But my heart still feels betrayed.

"When he's late coming back from the office, I wonder whether he's with her. When he looks at a woman, I wonder whether he would ask her out if he weren't with me. I used to enjoy it when other women looked at Paul. He's a very handsome man, and it made me proud to be with him and have other women checking him out. But now, when they look, I cringe. I don't have the secure feeling that I'm the only one."

It takes time to build trust into a relationship. Ideally, love and trust grow together, with trust being the strong foundation on which love is built. But events before and during the separation often shatter that trust. It may have been a secret you confided when you felt especially close that was later used against you. It may have been infidelity, or an action done intentionally to hurt you. Whatever happened that caused it to break down, now that you are together again, trust must be rebuilt. Building trust takes time, so be patient. Still, it is important that the two of you are able to discuss the boundaries of your relationship now so that you both know what you can count on. Do you both agree, for example, that you will be faithful to the other? If so, and if you still feel insecure but your partner hasn't given you a reason to doubt him, then consider seeing a therapist to help you work through issues that are more real for you than for your partner.

You Harbor Lingering Rage and Resentment

"If I'm supposed to be so happy, why do I still feel angry so much of the time?" This a heartfelt question asked by many reunited couples. Everything is supposed to be better now that your partner's back—especially if she's being more tender and affectionate, or doing thoughtful little things, trying to make up for the pain she's caused. This is the happy ending in which you are naturally expected to rejoice. Your friends congratulate you, your coworkers tell you they knew all along that things would work out, and your family heaves a sigh of relief. Yet you may wonder why you feel angry or resentful so much of the time.

Perhaps all is well at first, when passionate lovemaking keeps you feeling secure and fulfilled. But then you begin to remember past pain. "How could he have done this to me? How could he have hurt me this way? How could he have hurt our children? How could he make a fool of me, a mockery of our marriage?" Little by little, all the pain that you felt turns to anger and then to rage.

> Frances felt her anger grow in the first few weeks that Paul was back. In their quiet moments, when they were at dinner or watching television, she would sometimes look at him and think, "How could you have been so hateful to me in these past months? How could you have consciously set out to destroy our marriage? How could you have treated our love so carelessly, even trying to drive me away?"
>
> The intensity of her rage surprised and frightened her. She didn't want to be angry; she wanted to use all her energies to be loving and warm, and supportive of their renewed relationship. She wanted to nurture it like a newborn baby. But the rage would flare up without provocation. When she was cooking, she would suddenly be overwhelmed with anger at how Paul had refused to take her calls while they were separated. When she was driving to work, she would feel her stomach tighten as she thought of the pain she had experienced knowing of his infidelity. Her anger was threatening to overwhelm her.

Perhaps the worst part of rage is that it leaves you feeling guilty. You don't want to be angry all the time. You tell yourself that you "should" be happy, and you feel guilty about being angry. This may fuel your anger even further. You fear that if you express yourself, you're going to cause problems in the new relationship and sabotage it before it's had a chance to grow strong. Yet you can't help your feelings. As the rage wells up, all you can think about is what your partner put you through.

You need to express this anger in a productive way. Finding a therapist who can facilitate the safe release of your anger and help you resolve it would be an excellent investment. You may want to express it to your partner and have her understand that it's not directed at her—that you simply need to let go of your pent-up emotions—but before you do that, think about how it's going to serve the new relationship. The best way to handle sharing may be in a couples' support group, where both of you can be assisted to process your feelings.

You Fear the End of the "Honeymoon" Phase

When Paul began spending more time at work and less with Frances, she got nervous. "It was Paul's shutting me out of his life that caused all our problems before. Now, when he leaves for work before I'm even up, I think that he doesn't care as much. When he won't take a Saturday off to walk along the beach with me, as he did when we first got back together, I'm concerned that he doesn't want our relationship to work as much as I do. He tells me he's just busy and not to worry, that we'll have more time together soon, but I can't help it. After all, I'm taking time out of my day to do things for him, and I'm just as busy as he is."

When you first reconcile, you are usually both on your best behavior—doing little things to please the other and refraining from annoying habits that drive your partner up the wall. It's almost as if you are dating again. You spend time together doing fun things, enjoying each other's company, and basking in your newfound love. It's like a second honeymoon.

The honeymoon stage isn't permanent, however. Little by little, as you become accustomed to being together again, and you both feel more secure in your relationship, it's natural to start relaxing and slipping back into old habits. You might become a little less attentive, a little less supportive. Perhaps your partner buries himself at the computer again, or you fall back into some of those irritating habits, like always being late.

Does this mean the romance is gone? No. It simply means that your relationship has stabilized, and you are comfortable with each other again. When you reunite, it's easy to say that you will find ways to spend more time together and show your appreciation for each other. But often, those little loving gestures become fewer in number, and time spent together shrinks as the outside world starts to demand more attention and your partner is now "too busy" for you. It's easy to feel insecure when you are still doing thoughtful things for her, yet your partner has gone back to—as you see it—taking you for granted. To keep your relationship strong, use your newfound skills to find ways for each of you to fulfill the other's important needs in order to keep the romance and intimacy thriving. Above all, remember that relationships are works in progress and don't sweat the small stuff!

Making It Better This Time

The ways to maintain vitality and romance in your relationship are very much like the steps you took to bring you and your partner back together again. In Chapter 10, we'll discuss in greater detail how to sustain your relationship. The following points are especially important during the early stages of reconciliation.

Keep the Channels of Communication Open

Chances are, you are both experiencing many fears and apprehensions that you may be afraid to express or that your partner resists discussing. Read Chapter 8 with your partner. Practice the skills of good communication, invite her to share her feelings, and listen—or get outside help. Maintaining the open communication that started during the reunion process will be really important to truly closing the door on the past and to embracing your being back together—and your future.

Focus on the Present

You have absolutely no power over the past. No matter how much you think, hope, and pray, you are not going to change one minute of what has already happened. But you have a great deal of power over today, because you can decide what you are going to do, say, think, and feel.

A simple but powerful phrase to help you stay focused on the feelings and goals you're working toward is: "One Day at a Time." Clear your mind of past events, and the pain and unhappiness you went through, and focus only on the present. Remember that your big goal is made up of the small steps you take each day. When you're feeling anxious, ask yourself, "What can I do right now that is loving and will have a positive and productive payoff?"

Putting the past behind you is easier said than done. But there is an effective and fairly simple way to start. Listen to yourself, and be aware of what you are thinking and saying. You may not be conscious of how much you may be dwelling in the past. But when you begin to talk about it, stop! Make an effort to catch yourself. If you start to say, "When John left me, I . . ." Stop! Take a deep breath, and begin again. "Today I can . . ." Today is all that matters. Look toward the future. Do all you can to replace doubt with optimism.

Second, replace the past in your thoughts with something else. Refocus yourself. When that image of her with her former boyfriend flashes into your mind, replace it with the look on her face when she came toward you with her arms open, ready for a big hug. Instead of thinking of those nights apart, remember how wonderful it was the last time you were together. Plan a happy future and make it as detailed and vivid as possible.

Continue to Take Care of Yourself

During the separation stage, you worked at taking care of yourself. Continue to do that! Keep to that exercise plan and continue the classes you started. Just because your partner is back is no reason to stop caring for yourself. In order to have the best possible relationship, you want to be the best possible you. This will better equip you to handle any future problems. And do not stop going to group therapy or counseling just because your partner is back. Continue working toward being your personal best, and know that it is a real key to how happy you will be with your partner, and to how successful reconciling with your partner will be.

Maintain Your Outside Interests

Remember your other commitments, and don't make your relationship the only important thing in your life. Of course, you want to spend more time with your partner now, but continue to cherish the good friends who stood by you or the new friends you made during the separation. The temptation is to think that now that your partner is back, it's okay to let go of the things you've been doing, such as getting together with friends, or pursuing fitness, hobbies, and leisure activities. Not so! Merge the best of the old with the best of the new. While you were apart, you probably met new people and developed new interests and goals for yourself. Continue to include them in your life and keep working toward your goals.

Consider Counseling, Individually and as a Couple

If you were in counseling during the separation, now is not the time to quit. Continue your sessions. You'll have new, exciting, frustrating, and sometimes, painful experiences to discuss that a therapist can help you understand and work through. If your spouse is willing, get him into counseling with you. The two of you are taking those first steps to learning new ways of relating to and communicating with each other. An experienced professional who is skilled and objective can be of immense help at this time.

You struggled a long time to get to this point, but happy endings are only the beginning. Some of the problems that were there before the separation may still remain; others may be more obvious or have come to the surface. With good will on both sides, you can resolve some of the predictable frustrations you are likely to undergo. Remember, reuniting is a continuing process in sustaining a loving and lasting relationship.

Questions for Reflection

1. What worries still haunt you now that you are reconciling?

   _____

   _____

2. What communication or relationship tools have you acquired to help resolve issues?

   _____

   _____

3. How are you and your partner currently handling concerns that arise?

   _____

   _____

4. Have you and your partner considered counseling? What are the benefits of working with a counselor?

   _____

   _____

5. What resources will you continue to develop?

   _____

   _____

chapter *ten*

Sustaining a Loving and Lasting Relationship: Advice from Those Who've Been in Your Shoes

Now that you and your partner are back together, what will you do to make sure that you stay together? Successfully reunited couples tell us that getting back together is only the beginning. Sustaining their relationship—staying happy together—is a lifelong process. These couples have learned ten keys to sustaining a loving and lasting relationship. By committing to apply these ten essential keys, you are and your partner can create an unbreakable bond of intimacy and love.

ONE: Make Your Relationship a Priority

Your relationship should be your number-one priority; keep its well-being foremost in your mind. Think about how your decisions and interactions will affect the relationship as well as both of you as individuals. You may feel that you individually can survive poor communication, too little time spent together, or lack of fulfillment in areas of need. But can the relationship survive? The relationship has to be your number-one priority if it is to succeed.

If you're offered a promotion that requires a lot of travel, consider how it will affect the time you spend with your partner. If your sister wants to move in with you while she attends college, think about how it will affect the quality of your relationship.

When problems come up, sit down and discuss how they affect the relationship. Too often, conflicting needs or expectations are seen as win/lose struggles between partners. "If you get your way, I don't get mine." Instead, think of making the relationship the winner and ask, "How is what we're doing affecting our relationship?" "How can this be resolved in a way that works for the relationship?" It's okay to put the well-being of your relationship before the needs of others. You've worked very hard to reconcile—continue to make your relationship number one.

"Work used to be my number-one priority, even though I loved Carol," said Tom. "I also had family and social obligations that I felt I couldn't drop. But when we got back together, we both decided that the relationship had to come before everything else. I gave up a lot of outside activities that had just accumulated. Now we schedule regular time together when we'll sit down and talk, or go out and do something we like. We'll make it a point to touch base on the phone, especially when one or both of us is working late. We never let ourselves put other obligations ahead of sustaining our relationship."

TWO: Keep the Lines of Communication Open

The many couples profiled in this book all had one thing in common: a strong belief that the most important factor in successfully reuniting and sustaining a loving and lasting relationship was their emphasis on good communication. Time and again they told us, "Don't let the problems build up. Make time, every day, to share what's going on in your life. Don't talk just about the big, serious topics, but about the little, day-to-day ones, too. Express yourself clearly. No one is a mind reader; don't assume the other person knows what you're thinking. Talk, listen, and face the problems together. If you ignore them, they'll just get worse!"

Good communication is a two-way street. It requires the ability to state your needs clearly in a way that helps your partner understand you. And it involves active listening, in which you pay close attention to your partner's underlying feelings as well as the words being said.

> Since Carol still felt insecure about her husband's past infidelity with a coworker, Tom decided that if Carol had more information about what really went on in his business life, she would be less anxious. "I told Carol more about what I do, and the highlights and frustrations of my day. I also made a point of having her meet me at the office sometimes. As she became acquainted with my colleagues and got to know them as real people, she felt less threatened. When I began to share more of my day with her, Carol and I became closer, and she began to trust me more."
>
> Carol was thrilled with Tom's new openness. "The talking soon carried over into other areas as well. It was as if once Tom learned how to talk about his experiences at work, he was willing to go the next step and discuss other things, too. We talk about everything now, getting problems out into the open before they become really bad."

THREE: Lighten Up and Have Fun!

Put the fun back into your marriage. Remember all the little things that were fun and made you feel so connected when you first started dating? The spontaneous phone calls, the humorous cards, the impromptu dancing to the stereo, the inside jokes only the two of you shared? A relationship is not all heartfelt talks and serious moments. Part of the joy in being together is having fun. All too often, a couple focuses on the work and obligations, and loses the vibrancy that kept the relationship alive. Playfulness and laughter create those special memories that sustain you through the inevitable rough spots. Be sure to include time for fun as regularly as you schedule work commitments or other obligations. We think these moments just show up by themselves, but they need to be intentionally incorporated into a relationship. This is especially true as our lives get busier, and most especially after relationships have been tested by going through discord. Plan activities that can give the two of you respite from the day-to-day routines of life, and can breathe fun, joy, and laughter into your lives.

> "One of the reasons I fell in love with Carol," Tom said, "is that when I was with her, we were always laughing and having a good time. We did so many things. Then real life took over, and soon our lives were mostly about our work. When we got back together again, we both agreed that we needed to bring back the time we once took to enjoy ourselves, to simply go play and have fun. Now we schedule an activity a month in advance and enjoy anticipating it. Having a good time has brought us closer together."

FOUR: Remind Your Partner of Your Love—All the Time

Just as no one is a mind reader when it comes to problems in a relationship, no one is a mind reader for the good points, either. You love and appreciate your partner, so let him know it. Every day, remind both yourself and your partner of the love between you. Serve up a compliment first thing in the morning. Think how happy your partner will be to wake up and see your smiling face and hear, "I love you because . . ." That one compliment, that one reassurance, can set the tone for the whole day. Call your partner at work, or leave a loving message on the answering machine at home. Do thoughtful things for your partner, like bringing her a drink while she's watching TV or ironing his clothes for work. Even the worst day brightens when your partner reminds you of how much you're appreciated and loved. These things can seem small, but they can be the glue that reminds each of you that you're taking this journey together, being with each other through thick and thin—and that you want it this way. Small thoughtful acts can say, "I want you to be happy. I want to make you happy."

"I never used to be very verbal," Tom said. "I thought that Carol would just know how much I loved her. Now I make a point of saying 'I love you.' So rather than sound like a broken record, I say things like, 'I'm so happy I married you!' I want Carol to know how much I value our relationship, and I really appreciate it when she tells me how important it is to her, too."

FIVE: Keep Learning about How to Have a Happy Relationship

While you were apart, you probably haunted bookstores and chat rooms, looking for answers about what went wrong with your marriage and how to repair it. Like most separated partners, you searched for ways to understand what happened to destroy your relationship. Reading helped you analyze your feelings and recognize the workings of your relationship.

Now that the two of you are back together, you haven't stopped needing information about yourself and what's happening between you. You still can benefit from suggestions on how to resolve problems, old or new, and strengthen your relationship. Continue to read books and magazine articles. Share these with each other and discuss them. Attend a couples' retreat or communication seminar together. Applying the exercises and suggestions provided will keep your relationship fresh and interesting. When you see those little "how to know if he really loves" quizzes in magazines, read them together, using them as an opportunity to open up a conversation to talk and laugh about certain things in your relationship that fit and don't fit the quiz. The point is, never assume that you know all there is to know about what keeps a relationship happy and thriving. (At the back of this book is a list of suggested readings. You and your partner might enjoy going through several of the sections together and deciding which books would be helpful to you.)

"I got the idea to go to counseling from a book I read," Tom said. "I had always thought that counseling was only for people who are emotionally unstable, and that I would be seen as weak if I couldn't solve my own problems. Reading the book made me see how important it was that I understand myself if I wanted to understand someone else. And it gave me some practical ideas I could use right away. Now that Carol and I are reconciled, we're reading books together, and Carol has started going to counseling with me. It's good. We're exploring things we should have years and years ago."

SIX: Remember What You've Accomplished When Things Get Tough

When your new relationship hits a few rough spots—and it will—remind yourself of why you worked so hard at getting back together. What were your reasons? Just what is it about the relationship that made you go through everything you did in order to salvage the love? Remember your partner's good qualities—those that made her attractive in the first place. Think about the wonderful things that are happening to you right now. What nice things is your partner doing for you every day? What has he said or done lately that shows he loves and cherishes you? When she forgets to pick up the dry cleaning for what seems like the hundredth time, remind yourself that she never forgets to call you to tell you she loves you. When he complains about your mother's visit last weekend, remember that he also took the time to rearrange her furniture and paint her living room the week before. Focusing on what's right can help make what's wrong seem not quite so important.

"Tom still annoys me when he spends all day Sunday glued to his football games," Carol said, "but then I remember how much I look forward to his coming home from work each day because he really devotes that time to talking to me. Now whenever Tom is distracted by sports, I remind myself that it's really a small chunk of his time in comparison to what he spends with me. Tom will always love football, but I know now that he loves me even more."

SEVEN: Maintain Your Own Identity

To be complete, you need to find meaning outside of your partner, no matter how much you love him or her. When you are strong and fulfilled, you have things to share that make you interesting. You intrigue your partner as he finds that you have a lot more to offer than he ever suspected.

During your separation, you worked on gaining a sense of identity, on knowing who you are and what you want. Now that you know yourself better, continue to build on it. Find your own focus and keep it sharp. You set goals for yourself during the time apart; continue to work toward them now, and set new goals as you achieve old ones. Your partner will respect you for doing so, and you will strengthen the relationship.

Each of you should be independent and yet interdependent. Be certain that you have a life of your own, and that you could survive alone if you had to. Knowing that you have that option gives much more meaning to your decision to be together: You are together not out of desperation, not because you have to be, but because you want to be.

"When Tom left me, my standard of living really fell," Carol said. "I had been pretty casual about my job because Tom was doing so well. We really didn't need my money. When we were together, I used money I earned at work mostly for extras, like things around the house, gifts for family and friends, and clothes for myself. I enjoyed my work and the people around me, but I never took it seriously. I just figured Tom would always be there to take care of me. When he left, I had a pile of bills and was living in a condo that used up my paycheck. I had to take in a roommate to make ends meet. It really shook me up, and I decided I would never let myself get that dependent again. I started digging into my job and found out what I would have to do to advance. I've gotten one raise, and I'm due for another. Now that I know I can take care of myself, I feel a lot better about our relationship. I know I don't need Tom; I love him. When we got back together and started talking about remodeling our kitchen, I felt that my say really meant something."

EIGHT: Develop a Support System That's Rooting for the Relationship

During the separation, you leaned heavily on your support system. You spent long nights talking to friends and doing things with them to keep busy. Those support systems were vital to your survival and they still are. Don't give them up now that you and your partner are back together. But be careful that you have the right type of support system. Old friends may be feeling neglected now that you no longer need them as much, or they may believe you're making a mistake in reconciling. Some might even be jealous of your newfound happiness—especially if they are not in a good relationship of their own. Whatever the reason, these people can sabotage the relationship you are working so hard to maintain. Talk with them. Make it clear that you are fully committed and that you could use their support. Focus on friends who truly want you to succeed.

"My best friend, Fay, was there for me all during the separation," Carol said. "She cried with me, held my hand, listened to me for hours. When Tom and I got back together, she encouraged me every step of the way and seemed truly happy for me. Even though she said, 'I couldn't do what you're doing, but if this is what you want, then it's what you should do.' Tom's friend, Hal, was just the opposite. He made it very clear that he

> thought Tom was making a mistake coming home. Tom likes Hal, but rarely sees him anymore. We don't need the extra tension in our marriage at this stage. We want to be with friends who are rooting for us."

NINE: Be Best Friends with Each Other

Your friends are important to your well-being. Wouldn't it be wonderful if you always had your best friend at your side? Ideally, your spouse should be not only your lover and your coparent, but also your best friend. This is your lifelong companion. You and he will spend more time with each other than with anyone else. You will know each other in more ways than anyone else—companions in the adventure called life. When you think of your partner as your best friend, you treat each other accordingly. Consider how you act with the other friends you treasure, and treat your partner with the same courtesy, respect, and affection. Like many happily married people, you'll be happy to proclaim, "I married my best friend!"

> "I can truly say that Carol is now my best friend," Tom says. "I share all my deepest thoughts with her, and she supports me in all I do. I know that she'll always be there for me, through thick and thin. Our friendship sustains me during all the ups and downs of life. It's such a good feeling, especially on those days when the world is sitting on my head, so to speak. I think, I'll be so glad when this day is over. I'll go home to Carol and we'll have a great evening together. She is the light at the end of every tunnel."

TEN: Plan for Your Future Together

While it's important to focus on the day-to-day things you do together, it's also valuable to think about your future together. Imagine the good times that lie ahead. Think about next week, next year, five years from now. What do you look forward to sharing with your partner? Is it retirement and time to travel around the country? Do you dream of having children, or look forward to grandchildren? You put a lot into this relationship; what do you expect to get out of it? What do you fantasize about in those quiet moments when it's just the two of you together? Building dreams for the future gives you common goals to work toward. It focuses your energy on creating experiences you can share.

"The night I proposed to Carol, we talked about our future together," Tom said. "We saw ourselves in a small town, raising our children. In the middle of all our problems, while we were separated, I felt very sad that we weren't going to have that dream. Now that we are back together, we talk about it even more. It's something we share, something we can work toward. It brings us closer together, having a common goal."

Making the Ten Keys Part of Your Happy Marriage

Now that you've learned the top ten keys for sustaining a happy relationship, think about your own situation. How well are you and your partner doing these things? In what areas do you need to improve? As you did in previous chapters, review these steps together and set goals that will help you to improve in each of these areas. For instance, if you've stopped learning about ways to cultivate a happy marriage, set a goal to attend a couples' retreat together in the next six months. If there hasn't been much fun in your life lately, commit to making Friday nights your "fun night" and watch a silly movie together. (Don't forget to throw popcorn in each other's mouth!) You've devoted tremendous time and effort to repairing your relationship—don't let the fruits of your labor die from neglect.

Questions for Reflection

1. How are we continuing to keep the lines of communication open?

   _____

   _____

2. What am I doing to develop and maintain my own identity?

   _____

   _____

3. How have we brought more fun into our life as a couple?

   _____

   _____

4. When we go through rough patches, what qualities in my partner remind me of why I want to spend the rest of my life with him/her?

   _____

   _____

5. What are we doing so that we can continue to learn and grow?

   _____

   _____

chapter *eleven*

"A Miracle We're Together": One Couple's Journey from Separation to Reconciliation

The couples you've read about in this book are of all ages and walks of life. They separated for many different reasons. What they had in common was that they separated at some point in their relationship, resolved the problems that led to the breakup, and successfully got back together again. Sometimes their journey from a troubled relationship to separation and then back together took several months; sometimes it took much longer. For some, the separation created the impetus to grow and change, and then put their relationship back together. For others, getting back together occurred after they had divorced and lived separate lives. In the end, all found the strength and commitment to build a stronger and enduring relationship with their original partner. This chapter profiles Bill and Christy's journey from separation, to reconciliation, to finally being a happy couple. Their story shows us that successful reconciliation is possible if your separation is used as a time for learning, growth, and renewal, and if you bring to your new relationship a stronger self, better communication, and greater fulfillment of your needs. Throughout this book, we've examined the many ways that your separation can lead to a new and happier relationship. Let's take a look at how Bill and Christy went through this process.

Stage One: The Problems Mount

"When I look back, I can't believe how much things have changed." Christy's soft voice belied the intensity of her feelings as she recapitulated the events of the past year. "I thought for sure that Bill and I would never get back together again. We had been through so much, and we seemed to have so much going against us. It's a miracle that we're together."

Bill nodded in agreement. "I remember when we split up. I was drinking and spending money like it was going out of style. Our bills weren't getting paid, and I had to file for bankruptcy. I knew Christy had a hard time working and taking care of the house and the baby, but I didn't show her any consideration at all. I was really nasty to her and the baby—as if I was trying to get back at her for something, and I didn't even know what. I kept promising her I would change, but I never managed it for more than a few days. Then I just slid back into the same routine all over again. Finally, I really lost it one night, and Christy kicked me out. I felt as if I were going crazy—I couldn't sleep, I didn't know what to do. Fortunately, my boss saw what was going on and insisted I get help. I'll always be grateful because it really changed our lives."

Christy interrupted, "I could see how much Bill was hurting, but I couldn't seem to reach him. I thought a lot of our problems stemmed from his relationship with his father, an alcoholic. Every time his father called, he seemed to be able to make Bill feel guilty and worthless. No matter how much I told Bill I loved him and believed in him, it didn't seem to help. I was afraid I would end up in the same kind of marriage as his mother. Even though I was scared, I knew I had to do something."

Needs and Expectations

Relationships are like real-life dramas that feature main actors (you and your partner) and invisible participants (your needs and expectations).

Christy and Bill had gotten married after graduating from high school. Both were eager to leave homes marked by constant arguing, tension, and conflict. Bill was a sensitive young man who was especially glad to get away from the demands and put-downs of his father. Nothing he did was ever good enough, no matter how hard he tried. Christy's quiet personality and commonsense approach to life seemed just what he needed.

The couple experienced some problems during their first few years of marriage, but no more than other couples they knew. It wasn't until the birth of their daughter, Tessy, that major difficulties started to surface. As with many couples in troubled relationships, the birth of a child was an added strain. Christy was torn between quitting her job to stay home with Tessy and wanting to advance in her career. Bill agreed that Tessy's care was important, but pointed out that Christy's paycheck made the payments on the furniture and the entertainment system they had bought for their home.

He also felt resentful that Tessy now seemed to claim so much of Christy's attention. The quiet times they had spent together, the intimate moments, the talks late at night—all these seemed to have vanished. It was as if Tessy had taken his place as the most important member of the family.

Bill's own emotionally deprived childhood did not prepare him for being a nurturing parent. He was short-tempered and irritable when Tessy was crying or fussing. It was a major source of conflict between him and Christy—especially since Christy had promised herself that she would be the kind of loving mother to Tessy that her own mother had never been to her.

Most importantly, Bill was seeking to "relax" more and more by drinking with his friends and spending money on things they couldn't afford. When Christy confronted him, he would become belligerent and verbally abusive. The situation reached a crisis when Christy discovered that they would have to declare bankruptcy because of the extent to which Bill had been spending and trying to cover his debts with credit cards. When Bill dealt with the situation by going on a drinking spree, Christy decided to throw him out of the house.

Stage Two: Separation

"The night I told Bill to get out I wasn't sure what I was going to do, but I knew I had to do something. I just couldn't take it anymore. Our fights had escalated over the last three months to the point where it seemed we were screaming at each all the time. A lot of nights, Bill wasn't coming home until two or three in the morning, and I was terrified that he had passed out somewhere or had gotten into an accident. It was affecting Tessy, too. She was getting nervous and not sleeping well. When I took her to the babysitter, she would cry and hang on to me. I couldn't leave her alone with Bill because he was so irritable when he was drinking. I remembered how frightened I used to be when my parents fought, and I didn't want the same thing to happen to Tessy.

"I was scared, too. It seemed like my worst nightmare had come true. I had always promised myself that my marriage would be different from my parents'. And here I was—going through the same thing.

"I really loved Bill. He could be so tender and considerate. I remember he brought me flowers on our first date. No one had ever done that before. We used to talk for hours about our dreams and what we wanted to have in our lives. I trusted him and admired him—he really seemed to know what he wanted."

Trying to Make It Alone

"The day after Bill left, I was panic-stricken. I just didn't know how I was going to survive without him. I had depended on him for everything. It wasn't as if I didn't have a responsible job—I did. People relied on me at work. But in my private life, it was as if my brain turned off and I let Bill take over.

"Thank God I had my sister to talk to. We've always been very close, and she had gone through a similar situation in her own marriage a few years before. I think that for the first two or three weeks, I spent most of my time on the phone with her, or Tessy and I would go and spend the night at her house. She really helped me by listening and reassuring me that I could make it without Bill.

"Most of all, she supported my decision to separate. I was feeling so guilty—thinking that maybe if I had been a better wife, Bill wouldn't have needed to drink. She helped me see that Bill's drinking was his problem, not mine. I'll always be grateful for that."

Stage Three: Preparation

"When I started to get on my feet again, I realized that I had never had a chance to find out what I could do. I was so focused on being a perfect wife to Bill and a good mother to Tessy that I had forgotten all about me. Bill kept calling and saying he wanted to come home again, but it just didn't feel right to me. I didn't want to repeat all the turmoil of those last few months, and I was afraid he would just go back to his old behavior again. I knew that if I was ever going to get any self-confidence, I was going to have to prove to myself that I could make it without him.

"I bought a lot of books on relationships and read everything I could get my hands on. I also joined a support group for a while. Some of the things I learned about myself in the group really helped my self-confidence. Listening to other people's stories helped me put what was happening to me in perspective. I also got a lot of good practical ideas from the group, like how to handle Bill's visits with Tessy.

"One of my friends mentioned that Al-Anon was for family members of alcoholics. I wasn't sure if Bill was an alcoholic, although his drinking certainly caused problems in our lives, so I didn't want to go at first. I'm glad that I did because it helped me understand what was happening with Bill, and I let go of trying to fix him. It was a relief to be able to concentrate on taking care of myself and Tessy.

"What I found out I needed most in separating was just the time and space to get to know myself, to find out what kind of a person I was and what I really wanted. Even though it was tough being a single parent, with all the books I was reading and workshops I was taking, I felt I was growing by leaps and bounds. When Bill called, I still felt a little guilty, especially because he couldn't see Tessy as much as he wanted to, but I was determined to prove that I could make it on my own."

Christy: "What I Learned about Myself"

"Probably the most important thing I learned about myself was that I am a strong person, and I do have what it takes to make it in this world. I never really knew that before, so I didn't have the self-confidence that I have now. I always thought that other people could handle things better or were smarter than me. Now I know that I can take care of problems that come up. I have a lot more self-esteem.

"I also found out that I enjoy learning new things. Right now I've got so many books I want to read, I can't buy any more until I finish what I have. One thing I've definitely decided is that I'm going back to college to finish getting my degree. I dropped out when Bill and I got married because I wanted more time with him, but I've regretted it—especially when I got passed over for promotions. I know it won't be easy to go back to school, but I'm going to start, even if it takes me a long time to finish.

"Another thing I've learned about myself is that I'm good with people. I thought I'd be too embarrassed to talk in those support groups, but I surprised myself. I got in touch with a lot of issues and feelings that had been buried for years and let them out. I was really proud of myself, especially when somebody came up after a meeting and said that hearing about my experiences had really helped her see what was happening in her own life.

"I also found out that I was a lot better organized than I ever thought I could be. Being a single parent means that you're always juggling your time. It seems that I never have time for myself except for the hour between when I put Tessy to sleep and when I collapse into my own bed. But I've learned to write everything down and make sure that the important things get taken care of.

"I've also learned to handle money a lot better. I used to be one of those impulse buyers—my money used to just dribble away. Now I've got a lot more control over where my money goes. It's a nice feeling to know that I can pay all my bills!

"I know it sounds strange to say so, but I'm really glad I had that time to myself. I don't think I'd be the person I am now if I hadn't."

Bill: "What I Learned about Myself"

"I guess I never really knew how much Christy and Tessy meant to me until the night Christy told me to leave. I knew I was out of control—I never let Christy know how much I was drinking—but even though I kept promising to change, I couldn't seem to do it.

"After I moved out, I went through a really bad time. I was so down on myself. I moved in with a buddy from work, and the two of us just partied all the time. I don't know how I managed to hang on to my job. Finally, one night I got so drunk I thought I was going to die. I thought about Christy and Tessy, and I knew I wanted to live. So I called my brother and asked if I could stay with him and dry out."

Starting Recovery

"It was really rough the first few days. My brother and his wife were there with me every minute. They took me to my first Alcoholics Anonymous meeting.

I would never admit that I was an alcoholic before. It wasn't easy working on the AA program. There were things I had a lot of problems with, like learning to give up the need to control. I still have problems with that one. But I'm working on it. Christy can tell you that I'm making progress.

"What I also realized was that even though I hated the way my father treated my mother and us kids, I was doing the same thing to Christy and Tessy. My father always found fault with everything—nobody could ever please him. And he always put us down. One thing I've learned is that I probably won't ever get the love I want from him, and I just have to learn to accept that.

"The Adult Children of Alcoholics group that I'm going to has helped a lot there. It's made me realize just how much of my thinking and the way I used to act were shaped by growing up in an alcoholic household. I was so used to all the craziness that I didn't know what normal was. In a way, it's like being reborn. I'm starting all over again, and it feels great!

"Something else I've discovered is how I tend to sabotage myself. I know I'm smart, but whenever I get into a situation that's really good, whether it's at work or with Christy, I seem to mess it up. I don't know whether it's because my father always said I'd never amount to anything, or whether it's me, but I'm aware of it now."

Bill: "I Can Change"

"Probably the most important thing I've found out is that I can change. When I lost Christy and Tessy, my world fell apart. I knew I wanted to get them back and be a family again, and I was determined to do whatever it took. Christy didn't believe me at first—I know she was afraid I'd slip into the old habits. But I was determined to prove to her that things were different, that I was different."

Stage Four: Reconciliation

"It's true that I had a hard time believing that Bill had really changed. We had been through so much together, and he had made so many promises that he had broken. I told him that I'd believe him if he proved it to me with his actions—and he did.

"One of the things that used to bother me about Bill was how he treated Tessy. He would be so impatient with her to the point of her being scared of him. Now, he's a lot better. He plays with her in a way she can enjoy, and he's much more patient.

"Another problem we had was our finances. We were so deep in debt. Before Bill moved back, I insisted that we work out a budget and contact all of our creditors. Now I handle the money because we both agree that I'm better at it. We have a business meeting once a month to see how we're doing, and we've actually been able to start a savings account.

"Probably the biggest reason I agreed to get back together with Bill was the change in his attitude. We're friends now, and we respect each other. Instead of putting me down, he supports me in what I'm trying to do, and I do the same for him. When we have a concern, we'll talk things out instead of arguing.

"I had to go through changes, too. I knew it was important, if we were going to make it, for me to establish who I was and develop confidence in myself. I was unsure of Bill, but I was also unsure of myself. I needed to prove to myself that I could be self-sufficient and not have to rely on Bill to take care of me. Our whole relationship is so much better now—we're really partners in life!

"There wasn't any one reason that I decided to get back with Bill. It was a whole lot of things that made me change my mind. Most important maybe is that I learned I could trust him to do what he said he would do. I saw how different he was with Tessy; he stopped drinking, we got our finances together, and we really started to communicate with each other. When we have a problem, we sit down and talk about it. We're each other's best friends now, and I feel that whatever comes up, we can handle it."

Christy and Bill: "What We Want and Need Now"

"I used to think that if Bill really loved me, he would satisfy all my needs," Christy said, "and I used to blame him when he didn't. I know now that's not realistic. One thing I definitely learned during our separation was that I'm basically responsible for my own happiness."

"That's a big relief to me," Bill said. "When Christy expected me to know what she wanted without telling me, I felt a lot of pressure. I was never really sure how she'd react. Sometimes I'd do something thinking she'd like it, and she'd get upset because it wasn't what she wanted. Then I'd get mad and decide I wouldn't do anything. The fact that we're communicating so much better now means that I don't have to guess about things. I know what's important to Christy."

"One of my biggest needs now," Christy added, "is to finish my schooling. I want to get my degree so that I'm qualified to move up into management. It's going to take awhile, and I'll need Bill's help, but it's something I'm determined to do. Fortunately," Christy smiled, "Bill agrees it's just as important as I do."

As Bill and Christy's experience shows, when separation seems the only solution, you are faced with a crisis situation that brings great pain, but also offers an opportunity for growth and renewal. Being on their own forced Bill and Christy to look at themselves in new ways and find new solutions to their problems. When they did, they were able to come back together in ways that brought them the happiness and love they so greatly desired.

Right now, you may want your partner back so much that the idea you could take the time to work on yourself first seems impossible. But it is possible. Like the couples interviewed for this book that successfully reconciled, your perspective will change as you start discovering your own strengths and resources. Build on your strengths and remember why you are working on yourself—it's to give you the best possible opportunity for the strong, loving, wonderful relationship you deserve to have.

Questions for Reflection

1. What childhood experiences have affected how you and your partner relate to each other, and the needs and expectations you brought to your relationship?

    _____

    _____

2. How have you and your partner used your separation to deal with the problems you brought to the relationship? What did you learn about yourselves?

    _____

    _____

3. In what new ways are you and your partner planning to resolve future problems or possible recurrences of old ones?

    _____

    _____

4. What new appreciation do you have for each other that didn't exist before?

    _____

    _____

5. What signs have you seen from your partner that express his or her love and commitment to permanently change for the better?

    _____

    _____

chapter *twelve*

Making a Lifetime Commitment: Advice from Successfully Reunited Couples

Winter Is Over

The emotional icicles grew and grew.

I wanted her to go . . . she did.

And so began a long, painful, lonely eternity.

Time passed.

Then she called and said, "I don't need you anymore,

So let's be together . . . I accept you as you are."

So, here we are . . . together.

Living and loving, learning and growing . . .

Knowing who we are, and what we want.

Finally at peace,

With ourselves, and with each other.

My dearest Jeannie, love of my life,

Winter is over.

—by Lee Shapiro (a poem to his wife)

Moving Your Relationship from Winter to Spring

In a relationship, "emotional icicles" can indeed grow and grow until they appear impossible to thaw. Did your marriage collapse under the weight of the emotional icicles between you? As the wall of ice grows thicker and thicker, it lengthens the distance between you until you find yourselves far apart. But the ice need not be permanent; spring can come after a season of patience and hard work—especially if you have the right tools. As you have seen from the many examples of couples in this book, there is hope for a new season of life together. As you gain new perspective and grow during separation, the ice between you can thaw—revealing a beautiful new beginning beneath the frozen ground.

How do couples come through the emotional icicles between them? What can their experience teach you about moving your own relationship out of winter and into spring? Let's take a look at couples whose stories are a reminder that no matter how great the difficulties seem, with time, effort, patience, and the power of forgiveness, it is possible to resurrect a seemingly lifeless relationship and create a new one that is warm and vibrant. Use what feels right to you from their examples as encouragement and guidance for your own situation.

Larry and Janice: "After Twenty-two Years of Marriage . . ."

Larry and Janice were typical of couples that had a deep underlying love for each other, but whose relationship was so chaotic that it seemed the only solution was separation. Some relationships spin so out of control that breaking up seems not only inevitable, but also desirable. Coming from alcoholic and emotionally abusive homes, both Larry and Janice continually struggled with issues of trust, dependency, fidelity, and control.

"I was the biggest victim who ever lived," Janice said. "But after twenty-two years of marriage, I decided to do something about it. I told Larry I was going to leave him in California and go back to Kansas City to find out who I really was. Amazingly, we stayed friends through all the fights—Larry even helped me with the move. Besides, on another level, I knew we loved each other, and hoped we would get back together again. But I also knew I had to leave so that things could change."

"Despite my outward behavior when Janice moved to Kansas City, inside I was lonely, confused, and angry after she left," Larry said. "I told myself I had no intention of ever reuniting. In time, the first of many girlfriends moved in. At that point, I felt my filing for divorce was just a matter of time."

"I didn't think I could stand to live alone, or support myself on my own," Janice said. "It was a struggle at first, but within a few months I had an apartment, a good job, and was beginning to piece together a social life. My job had a lot of responsibility, and my boss gave me lots of positive feedback, so that was a relief, and very reassuring. I felt self-confident for the first time in my life, and I found I really didn't need to depend on Larry in the ways I'd needed to before. But deep down, I also knew that Larry and I were good together. In spite of everything, we were still the best of friends, and he'd not asked for a divorce. About a year later, I called him up and told him I wanted to see if we could rebuild our relationship."

"Her call caught me by surprise," Larry said. "I was both very happy and reluctant at the same time. During the time Janice was gone, I had learned a lot about myself, especially through the eyes of some of the women I'd dated. They didn't put up with my being as judgmental, intolerant, and impatient as I was, so I had to work on those things. As I did, I got comfortable with myself, and didn't feel I needed someone else to 'complete' me, I learned to enjoy and appreciate my own company. Basically, I gave up womanizing and settled down. So when Janice called, I felt we had something to work on now, because we had both grown a lot."

"Nothing Is More Important than the Relationship!"

Larry said, "We've always been best friends, and we enjoy being together. We can sit and read for hours on end and not say a word; we just commune. What made our reunion work was that we decided nothing was more important than our relationship!"

When relationships deteriorate to the point that leaving seems the only solution, each partner tends to blame the other for their problems. "If only you did, or didn't do, this or that, our relationship would be okay," they think. When couples separate, they have a chance to focus on their own needs and responsibilities. With no one else to blame for their unhappiness, they are forced to look within themselves and discover how their own actions may be affecting their relationships and their lives.

Larry and Janice learned during their separation that there were really three entities in their relationship: "you," "me," and "the relationship." They recognized that if their relationship was to survive and grow, the emphasis needed to be on all three. There's an enormous difference between saying, "This is what you should do to make our relationship better," and saying, "This is what we could do to improve things." Larry and Janice's story shows us that couples that successfully reunite place the relationship first.

Barry and Darlene: "Building Up Instead of Tearing Down"

"Now we're building up our relationship instead of tearing it down," Barry declared, as he and Darlene discussed the new life they had created after reconciliation. Watching how comfortable they were together, it was hard to believe the couple had once experienced so much pain.

When you're first separated, there is a tendency to think of the situation as temporary. You hope to reunite as soon as possible. The prospect of being apart for months seems unmanageable. That you might be separated for years before coming together again seems truly unthinkable. Barry and Darlene were separated for four years before they reconciled.

Although drinking and drugs were a way of life for both of them during their marriage, Darlene's turning point came when her beloved brother was killed in an accident. "It was a wake-up call for me," she said about starting recovery from alcohol abuse. But Barry did not join her—he left, telling her to get on with her life so she wouldn't be "dragged down" by him. Darlene was devastated. Barry spiraled downward for three more years. Finally, he said, "I entered a rehabilitation program because I realized I had two choices: I could die, or I could change." During this time, in the back of her mind, Darlene hoped that Barry would get his life together so that they could reunite. But when he left the rehabilitation program and contacted Darlene, telling her he had changed and asking her to marry him again, she remembered his past behavior and said, "Prove it!"

Actions Speak Louder than Words

Like many partners in addictive relationships, Darlene had been disappointed so many times by unkept promises that she wasn't willing to risk taking any more chances. She didn't want to hear promises; she wanted to see Barry's words actually borne out by his actions. So she told him what she wanted. "I want a new engagement ring to symbolize a new and enduring commitment, and I want to see an attitude that shows I'm not being taken for granted anymore."

A year later, at Darlene's birthday party, Barry insisted she open his gift first. An engagement ring was inside—and as all the guests watched, Barry formally proposed to Darlene once more. He had settled his financial obligations, his new business was starting to prosper, and it looked as if they would even be able to buy a house soon. He had done what he had promised.

Making a Lifetime Commitment

When there have been long-term, major traumas, it's natural to continue to feel uncertainty for a while. During the first year, Darlene still harbored a lot of doubts. Barry had had so many problems that she wasn't sure he could really change permanently. Barry was aware of the difficulties. "I knew I had to be really sure I could make a lifetime commitment to myself to get and keep my life in order so that I could commit to Darlene," he said. "During the time I was in rehab, I made peace with myself and initiated change. I committed to staying sober and working a recovery program for life—which is key to my being able to commit to recreating a loving and healthy new relationship with Darlene."

"We Listen to Each Other Now—Trust Can Be Mended!"

Really listening to your partner is one of the greatest gifts you can give. It says, "You're important, and what you're feeling and thinking matter to me."

Barry found out the importance of listening because he really wanted Darlene back. "We don't keep things in anymore," he continued. "We listen to each other and don't take each other for granted. I used to lie to cover up for using drugs. Now, I no longer feel a need to lie to Darlene about anything." Darlene nodded in agreement, "I never have reason to doubt anymore—trust can be mended!"

Talking, Planning, and Working Together

Barry and Darlene's story shows us that, whatever the problems your relationship has experienced, it can get better. However troubled, relationships can be healed. They can go from devastating and traumatic to loving and fulfilling if both partners work to restore trust and communication.

"We've made huge strides in the last few years," Darlene continued. "The romance is back again. We go out with friends, but we also make certain to take a day, or an evening a week, just for ourselves. We've put the fun back in our marriage. Before, we never did anything. Now we walk along the beach, we make plans, we talk about goals, and we actually work toward those goals together. We're talking, planning, and pulling together."

Jay and Peggy: "We Decided to Reunite"

Of all the traumas that couples face, infidelity is one of the most painful. It strikes at the very heart of our self-esteem and our sense of sensuality and sexuality. The shock of betrayal and broken trust is profound, especially when one partner is totally unaware of the other's betrayal.

"We had just come back from a dinner when Peggy told me she was involved with someone else," Jay stated. A successful businessman, he'd thought he had a happy marriage and begged his wife to start marriage counseling. But when his wife refused to stop seeing the other man, he moved out. "I've been very lucky all my life," Jay said. "I was very successful and well-known in the community. It was extremely painful to tell my family and friends that my marriage had 'failed.'

"I was feeling a lot of hurt and anger," he continued, "but I loved our child, and I decided to support Peggy in any way I could. When her new boyfriend turned out to have problems of his own, I arranged for her to get counseling. I still had hopes that we would get back together, although they were extremely slim. My goal was to get my life in order and move forward.

"Almost a year after we split up, I got a call from Peggy. She wasn't happy with the man with whom she had been living, and it wasn't working out. During therapy, Peggy had been learning a lot about herself and what she needed, and she wanted to talk about the possibility of reconciling. We decided to start counseling together, but continued to live apart and not see anyone else. After two months, we decided to reunite."

Forgiveness and Commitment

The devastation and feelings of betrayal caused by infidelity are great, requiring enormous dedication and strengthening of your inner resources to reach the point where you can detach yourself from the pain and forgive. Continuing fears of recurrence can keep haunting you and take time, patience, and the development of trust to dissolve. It is a gradual process that takes time and the commitment of both partners.

Jay stated it well when he said: "There's a tremendous amount of forgiveness that has to take place and commitment to what you're going to do. I had a lot of fears about whether Peggy would really put the family first, and there are still events that trigger bad feelings about what happened while we were separated.

"Communication is really the key," Jay said. "We sit down together and make plans: for us individually and as a family. One of the things that worked best for us was to go away for a whole weekend and set goals. We decided to make a written plan, so that we would both know our goals and expectations. We make it a point to get together for lunch regularly to see how we're doing. We also make time for just the two of us to take walks, explore the neighborhood, go on weekly dinner dates, etc."

Jay and Peggy's experience shows us that you can rebuild a marriage after infidelity. As Peggy learned during therapy, her infidelity was just a symptom of greater problems within herself. When she learned more about her needs and the reasons for her betrayal, she was able to communicate better and have her needs met within her marriage. She and Jay rebuilt a true partnership and no longer fear that Peggy will seek satisfaction outside of her marriage.

Mindy and Steve: "Totally Committed Forever"

In Mindy's case, things culminated during a one-year period in which her husband, Steve, lost his job and was unable to get another one while her new fashion-accessory business zoomed to instant success. It was the final blow to a nineteen-year marriage that was already in severe difficulty. Steve had been demanding and verbally abusive for a long time. Mindy suspected he was involved with a coworker. She felt unhappy, downtrodden, and suffocated.

When Mindy tried to manage her stress by taking classes one night a week, Steve said that she was ignoring him and threatened to leave. Although she tried to buy peace by promising not to take any more courses, inwardly she rebelled. She went off to a weekend retreat. As he had threatened, Steve left. But both partners started to cry as Mindy told Steve, "It's no good. We've got to release each other.

"After Steve left, I was so happy and relieved," Mindy said. "I felt as if a ten-million-pound weight had been lifted from my shoulders. I went shopping, I talked on the phone for hours, I read in bed till three A.M.—all the things Steve had never allowed me to do. I thought, 'The world is so wonderful—why didn't I do this a long time ago?' It was an amazing, incredible period. I didn't want to get back together again—it was the last thing I wanted! But at the same time, I was sad. I felt intense sorrow because I really loved Steve, and he was still a part of me."

"He Started to Share His Feelings"

Mindy said, "A few days before my fortieth birthday, Steve called. He asked if he could take me out to celebrate. I had lost weight and wore a new outfit. He seemed to notice me for the first time and told me how beautiful I looked. After that, we started seeing each other and having wonderful times. I was so happy that we could still be friends. After a few dates, Steve revealed that he had been seeing someone else while we were married—even while we were in counseling! He wanted me to know that although he went through the motions, he hadn't really been trying during our marriage, and for the first time, he started to share his feelings with me. (He was seeing a psychologist, so I think that helped him talk.) I went crazy and told him, 'You have to decide whether you want her, or me!' That night, I knew we were going to try again."

"It's Okay to Be Vulnerable"

"Since then," Mindy continued, "we've done a lot of talking together. Over the next few months we shared things that happened over the last twenty years. We went through layer after layer after layer—until we got to the core. I felt very insecure about the possibility of his going back to the other woman, but I've worked through that now. One of the most frightening things was that I had left the marriage and found out I could make it, and now I was giving up some of that independence and becoming vulnerable again. But I've learned that it's okay to be vulnerable."

"We Have Unconditional Love"

"We have a strong partnership now," Mindy said. "If I come home and he sees I'm tired, he doesn't expect dinner. He doesn't watch as many hours of sports on TV anymore, either. I'm taking classes in the morning now instead of at night. We're spending time with each other and enjoying each other's company. We also give each other space to be alone; we don't smother each other. And we try not to make judgments about each other anymore. We really have an unconditional love now. It's something I've always wanted—I just never dreamt I could have it with Steve!"

Steve and Mindy's story shows us that separation can break the seemingly endless cycle of unresolved conflicts that can build up in a marriage. Steve resented Mindy's success and wanted greater control over her life. Mindy chafed at Steve's manipulation and relished her sense of freedom when they split up. It took a separation for Steve and Mindy to break through their old ways of relating to each other. Through therapy, personal growth, and honest communication, they were able to support each other instead of creating conflict. Without their separation, they would never have had the opportunity to work on themselves, enabling them to reunite in a way that allowed them to be true to themselves.

Pam and Gabe: "I Wasn't Willing to Throw Our Life Away"

Gabe and Pam had just celebrated their thirty-fifth wedding anniversary. Less than six weeks later—right after he returned from his high-school reunion—Gabe began an affair with his old high-school sweetheart.

"He just packed and left with no explanation and no warning," Pam recalls. "I came home from work one day and found a note on the table that said, 'I hope some day you'll forgive me.' That was all.

"I went into total shock—it was so completely unexpected and the last thing I would ever have imagined him doing. We were looking forward to retirement and talked often about how we wished to spend our time. It felt like he was leaving all of us—me, our children, and our grandchildren. It was devastating. A few days after he left, he called, but couldn't explain why he had left or what was really wrong.

"Three months later, just as unexpectedly, Gabe called and said, 'I'm coming back.' At that point I was feeling so brokenhearted that I agreed, but I insisted we see a psychologist. It was extremely helpful to both of us. In counseling, he learned better ways to deal with the stress he was experiencing and started to feel a lot better.

"At the time he left, Gabe was under tremendous work stress. It was causing some serious medical problems that were affecting his mood. He was on a downward spiral. There was a point after he returned where his health got so bad from the nervous tension that I lost all my anger toward him. I realized that his affair was a symptom of the painful struggles going on inside him—basically, he was trying to escape reality. I didn't know Gabe was so miserable. He kept everything inside until it just erupted.

"A lot of women wouldn't have given him a second chance, but we had three terrific children and five grandchildren who just loved their grandpa. I just wasn't willing to lose all the years we had invested in creating a family, and building a home and a life together. I wasn't willing to throw our life away! And I do know my children are grateful that I didn't kick him out for good.

"Separation, while painful, had a silver lining for me. When Gabe and I were first married, we had three children within seven years. I stayed home and raised my family the way most women did in the fifties. When Gabe left, I remembered how I'd always wanted to start a small catering business. And that's exactly what I did during our separation. It's been challenging, but a lot of fun—and I'm not about to give it up—not yet, at least!

"So my advice to anyone who finds themselves in a similar situation is, If you feel you still want your partner back, make a plan, work toward it, but by all means, have your own life, too!"

Pam and Gabe's story demonstrates the dangers of poor communication. Pam didn't know that for years Gabe had been under extreme stress until it culminated in an affair. Gabe had no idea that Pam had career aspirations of her own. Now that Pam and Gabe speak openly and honestly about their needs, they no longer fear that unexpressed needs and desires will create a wedge between them.

The Road to a Successful Reunion

As these stories show, each couple is unique, yet in many ways couples are the same. Relationships, whether of two or twenty-four years, follow similar stages on their way through breakup and reconciliation. During an unhealthy relationship there is usually disappointment, anger, fear, resentment, apathy, and trauma. After a breakup the partners each experience pain, doubt, anxiety, self-knowledge, and growth. After reconciliation come renewal, vitality, commitment, partnership, and love.

Seeking answers, each couple in our book made their way through the rough terrain of separation or divorce. Although the events leading to the breakup and the external solutions differed, the results of successful reunions were the same. Self-examination and self-knowledge, and development of a sense of identity and personal responsibility, led to the internal growth that allowed the partners to come back into revitalized relationships.

The strength, confidence, and self-awareness these couples gained from struggling with difficult emotions made them confident enough to risk becoming vulnerable, and to explore their relationship honestly. Their hard-won self-knowledge, and the desire to heal the wounds and reunite, enabled them to communicate openly with their partner. Most of all, they were able to place the focus of their attention on the relationship, and to make a commitment to their future together.

What Successfully Reunited Couples Want You to Know

Let's take a closer look at what these couples and others who have successfully reunited can teach you about how to rebuild your relationship.

Develop Your Own Identity

When we interviewed the couples whose stories you have read, they stressed over and over again the importance of developing a sense of your own identity. Kim expressed it best when she said,

"You have to feel good about yourself before others, including the people closest to you, will like you or respect you."

"You have to take a real good look at yourself, and see where the problem is, and correct it in yourself first," Darlene said. "Don't lose your own sense of self. I loved Barry so much that I relied on him for happiness, rather than myself. Believe in yourself—anything can happen if you truly want it!"

"When I regained confidence, Robert became interested again," Kim said. "All the time I was afraid he was going to leave me, so I clung tighter, but it only drove him further away. When he realized he wasn't the center of my life and that I had other interests, he wanted me."

The wife of an extremely wealthy man said, "Find your own identity and sense of worth. Look for something you're interested in and you can accomplish. It's very degrading to beg for money, and it builds up resentment."

"Know who you are and what you want, and know who the other person is and what he wants—then work together," Cheryl stated. "That sounds very practical, but it works. Treat your relationship as an investment—as a life goal."

Commit to the Relationship

Make your new relationship your highest priority. In making decisions, ask yourself, "How will this affect my relationship?" Commit to working on your partnership every day.

"Don't sell your relationship short—take your commitment seriously," Jay said. "The bottom line is that no relationship is perfect—each has its own set of problems. So focus on your needs and communicate them to the other person."

"It's worth the effort—you get out of it what you put into it," Cheryl said. "We've put a lot into our relationship, and the rewards have been tremendous!"

Communicate

Poor communication can kill a relationship; improved communication can revive it. Resolve not to fall back into old patterns of suppressing your thoughts and avoiding discussion. Keep the channels of communication open at all times.

"Talk, communicate," Carol said. "Face the problems right away, because you'll have to deal with them eventually anyway."

"Now that there's trust in the relationship," said Kim, "we communicate before things get out of hand."

Don't Sweat the Small Stuff

No relationship will ever be perfect. Let the little irritations go. Accept them as part of your partner's make-up—the person you fell in love with, warts and all. Don't let minor irritants get under your skin.

> "You can't change people. You have to work around things that bother you. We all have little habits that irritate others," Julie said.

> "A lot fewer things bother me now," said Katie. "There are very few things in life that are worth getting upset about."

Share the Responsibility

When both partners are working, sharing the responsibility for the home is important, too. Larry and Janice not only run their business together, but also enjoy doing their shopping, cooking, and cleaning jointly. Sunday mornings, Larry prides himself on his gourmet brunches. When you work together, even chores can be fun!

> "Share the problems and learn to be involved together," Carol said. "Instead of blaming, say, 'This is something we need to deal with together.'"

Strengthen Your Faith

Develop your beliefs or find sources of renewal that continue to strengthen you as you create your new relationship. A shared faith can be a greater source of connection between you and your partner, and provide opportunities for mutual activities and spiritual growth.

"If I didn't have my faith in God, I wouldn't be here today. He pulled me through more than one bad situation," said Darlene.

"God's not going to give you any more than you can handle," Carol said. "I believe that strongly."

Be Best Friends

A wonderful bonus of being in a deeply committed relationship is that you have a best friend as well as a partner. You can tell your spouse your deepest thoughts without fear of disapproval or criticism.

"Friendship is the most important thing," Katie stated. "I don't think you can have a long-term love relationship without friendship. It's the added dimension of trust and acceptance."

Think Positively

Problems are still going to arise. Troubles are a part of life. Take comfort in the fact that you and your partner can see things through together. Be optimistic about overcoming difficulties with your partner by your side.

"If you're having a bad day, find a way to get through it. Tell yourself, 'This, too will pass. Tomorrow will be better,'" said Amanda.

Would We Do It Again?

When couples were asked whether they would go through the reconciliation process again, they were unanimous in saying it was well worth it. However, most said they would wait longer to reconcile if they had to do it over again. Darlene spoke for all of them when she said, "Don't be in such a hurry to get together again. Looking back, I should have stayed on my own a little longer."

Partners who have an underlying love can bridge almost any gap. As you go through the peaks and valleys of separation and reconciliation, remember that the reward at the end is reunion with the person you love. Keep your eye on that goal; others have accomplished it, and you can, too. As Larry and Janice said, "If we hadn't gone through what we went through, we wouldn't be here today. Our marriage has never been better. We value it because we almost lost it."

Some separations were as short as two months, others as long as four years. Some partners had marriages or affairs in between the breakup and the reunion. A few had a child with someone else. Regardless of the obstacles, when self-searching and inner growth were combined with a deep bond of love, these partners were able to overcome old problems and find their way back to a mutually loving relationship. Isn't that what you want for you and your partner?

Questions for Reflection

1. How has your commitment to the relationship changed from the way it was before your separation to how it is now that you are reconciled?

   _____

   _____

2. What are each of you doing to keep the relationship strong now that you are back together?

   _____

   _____

3. What are each of you doing to maintain the trust that has been built?

   _____

   _____

4. In what ways are you stronger now than you were before the separation?

   _____

   _____

5. What have you learned about yourself that you didn't know before?

   _____

   _____

Suggested Reading

Surviving Separation

Chapman, Gary. *Hope for the Separated: Wounded Marriages Can Be Healed* (Chicago: Moody Publishers, 1996).

Fisher, Bruce, Ed.D., and Robert E. Alberti, Ph.D. *Rebuilding When Your Relationship Ends* (Atascadero, CA: Impact Publishers, 1999).

Hazvey, Donald R. *When the One You Love Wants to Leave* (Grand Rapids, MI: Baker Books, 1993).

Kingma, Daphne Rose. *Coming Apart: Why Relationships End and How to Live Through the Ending of Yours* (York Beach, ME: Conari Press, 2000).

Smalley, Gary, and Dr. Greg Smalley. *Winning Your Husband Back Before It's Too Late* (Nashville, TN: Thomas Nelson Publishers, 1999).

Smalley, Gary, Dr. Greg Smalley, and Deborah Smalley. *Winning Your Wife Back Before It's Too Late* (Nashville, TN: Thomas Nelson Publishers, 1999).

Wanderer, Zev, and Tracy Cabot. *Letting Go: A 12-Week Personal Action Program to Overcome a Broken Heart* (New York: Dell, 1987).

Personal Growth While Separated

Adrienne, Carol. *Find Your Purpose, Change Your Life* (New York: Harper Collins, 1999).

Cameron, Julia, and Mark Bryan. *The Artist's Way: A Spiritual Path to Higher Creativity* (New York: G. P. Putnam's Sons, 1995).

Covey, Stephen R. *The Eighth Habit: From Effectiveness to Greatness* (New York: Free Press/Simon & Schuster, 2004).

Ellis, David B. *Falling Awake: Creating the Life of Your Dreams* (Rapid City, SD: Breakthrough Enterprises, 2000).

Ford, Debbie, Neale Donald Walsch, and Jeremiah Abrams. *The Dark Side of the Light Chasers: Reclaiming Your Power, Creativity, Brilliance, and Dreams* (New York: Riverhead/Penguin Putnam, 1999).

Jeffers, Susan. *Feel the Fear...and Beyond: Mastering the Techniques for Doing It Anyway* (New York: Ballantine, 1998).

O'Grady, Dennis. *Taking the Fear Out of Changing* (Avon, MA: Adams Media Corporation, 1994).

Richardson, Cheryl. *Life Makeovers: 52 Practical & Inspiring Ways to Improve Your Life One Week at a Time* (New York: Broadway Books, 2000).

Waite, Linda J., and Maggie Gallagher. *Why Married People are Happier, Healthier, and Better Off Financially* (New York: Broadway Books, 2000).

Youngs, Bettie B., Ed.D., Ph.D. *Taste Berry Tales: Stories to Lift the Spirit, Fill the Heart and Feed the Soul* (Deerfield Beach, FL: Health Communications, Inc., 1999).

———. *Gifts of the Heart: Stories That Celebrate Life's Defining Moments* (Deerfield Beach, FL: Health Communications, Inc., 1999).

Youngs, Bettie B., Ed.D., Ph.D., Linda Fuller, and Donna Schuller. *Woman-to-Woman Wisdom: Inspiration for REAL Life* (Nashville, TN: Thomas Nelson, 2005).

Creating a Strong, Loving Relationship

Fowers, Blaine, J. *Beyond the Myth of Marital Happiness: How Embracing the Virtues of Loyalty, Generosity, Justice, and Courage Can Strengthen Your Relationship* (San Francisco: Jossey-Bass, 2000).

Gottman, John, and Nan Silver. *The Seven Principles for Making Marriage Work* (New York: Three Rivers Press, 1999).

Hendrix, Harville. *Getting the Love You Want: A Guide for Couples* (New York: HarperPerennial, 1990).

McGraw, Phillip C. *Relationship Rescue: A Seven-Step Strategy for Reconnecting with Your Partner* (New York: Hyperion, 2000).

Schnarch, David Morris. *Passionate Marriage: Love, Sex, and Intimacy in Emotionally Committed Relationships* (New York: Henry Holt, 1998).

Smalley, Gary. *Secrets to Lasting Love* (New York: Simon & Schuster, 2000).

Taylor, Maurice, and Seanna McGee. *The New Couple: Why the Old Rules Don't Work and What Does* (New York : Harper-Collins, 2000).

Tessina, Tina B., and Riley K. Smith. *How to Be a Couple and Still Be Free* (Franklin Lakes, NJ: New Page Books, 2002).

Separation and Reconciliation

Chapman, Gary D. *Hope for the Separated: Wounded Marriages Can Be Healed* (Chicago: Moody Press, 1996).

Christensen, Andrew, and Neil Jacobsen. *Reconcilable Differences* (New York: Guilford Press, 2000).

Davis, Laura. *I Thought We'd Never Speak Again: The Road from Estrangement to Reconciliation* (New York: HarperCollins, 2002).

Markman, Howard J., Scott M. Stanley, and Susan L. Blumberg. *Fighting for Your Marriage: Positive Steps for Preventing Divorce and Preserving a Lasting Love* (San Francisco: Jossey-Bass, Inc. 2001).

Talley, Jim. *Reconcilable Differences: Healing for Troubled Marriages* (Nashville: Nelson, 1991).

Weiner-Davis, Michele. *The Divorce Remedy: The Proven 7-Step Program for Saving Your Marriage* (New York: Simon & Schuster, 2001).

Healing after Infidelity

Carter, Dave. *Recovering from Extra-Marital Affairs* (Chicago: Moody, 1992).

Farbman, Suzy. *Back from Betrayal: Saving a Marriage, a Family, a Life* (South Boardman, MI: Crofton Creek Press, 2004).

Glass, Shirley P., with Jean Coppock Staeheli. *Not "Just Friends": Rebuilding Trust and Recovering Your Sanity after Infidelity* (New York: Free Press, 2003).

Schneider, Jennifer P. *Back from Betrayal: Recovering from His Affairs* (San Francisco: Harper & Row, 1988).

Spring, Janice Abrahms, with Michael Spring. *After the Affair: Healing the Pain and Rebuilding Trust When a Partner Has Been Unfaithful* (New York: HarperCollins, 1996).

———. *How Can I Forgive You?* (New York: HarperCollins, 2004).

Youngs, Bettie B. Ph.D., Ed.D. *Woman-to-Woman Wisdom: Inspiration for REAL Life* (Nashville, TN: Thomas Nelson, 2005).

Healing the Family Unit

Knox, David, with Kermit Leggett. *The Divorced Dad's Survival Book: How to Stay Connected with Your Kids* (New York: Insight Books, 1998).

Lansky, Vicki. *Divorce Book for Parents: Helping Your Children Cope with Divorce and Its Aftermath* (New York: New American Library, 1989).

Lasher, M. *My Kind of Family: A Book for Kids in Single-Parent Families* (Burlington, VT: Waterfront Books, 1991).

Marston, Stephanie. *The Divorced Parent: Success Strategies for Raising Your Children after Separation* (New York: William Morrow and Company, Inc., 1994).

McGregor, Cynthia. *The Divorce Helpbook for Teens* (Atascadero, CA: Impact Publishers, 2004).

Stahl, Philip Michael. *Parenting after Divorce: A Guide to Resolving Conflicts and Meeting Your Children's Needs* (Atascadero, CA: Impact Publishers, 2000).

Wallerstein, Judith S., and Sandra Blakeslee. *What About the Kids? Raising Your Children Before, During, and After Divorce* (New York: Hyperion, 2003).

Youngs, Bettie B., Ed. D., Ph.D. *Safeguarding Your Teenager from the Dragons of Life: A Guide to the Adolescent Years* (Deerfield Beach, FL: Health Communications, Inc., 1998).

———. *Living the 10 Commandments in NEW Times* (Deerfield Beach, FL: Faith Communications, Inc, 2004).

Youngs, Bettie B., Ed.D., Ph.D., and Jennifer Youngs. *Taste Berries for Teens: Inspirational Short Stories and Encouragement on Life, Love, Friendship and Tough Issues* (Deerfield Beach, FL: Health Communications, Inc., 1999).

————. *A Teen's Guide to Living Drug Free* (Deerfield Beach, FL.: Health Communications, Inc., 2003).

————. *A Taste-Berry Teen's Guide to Managing the Stress and Pressures of Life* (Deerfield Beach, FL: Health Communications, Inc., 2001).

————. *A Taste-Berry Teen's Guide to Setting & Achieving Goals* (Deerfield Beach, FL: Health Communications, Inc., 2002).

————. *Taste Berries for Teens Journal: My Thoughts on Life, Love and Making a Difference* (Deerfield Beach, FL: Health Communications, Inc., 2000).

————. *More Taste Berries for Teens: A Second Collection of Short Stories and Encouragement on Life, Love, Friendship and Tough Issues* (Deerfield Beach, FL: Health Communications, Inc., 2000).

————. *Taste Berries for Teens #3: Inspirational Short Stories on Life, Love, Friends and the Face in the Mirror* (Deerfield Beach, FL: Health Communications, Inc, 2002).

————. *Taste Berries for Teens #4: Inspirational Short Stories on Being Cool, Caring and Courageous* (Deerfield Beach, FL: Health Communications, Inc., 2004).

————. *365 Days of Taste Berry Inspiration for Teens* (Deerfield Beach, FL: Health Communications, Inc., 2003).

Communication

Bernstein, Jeffrey, and Susan Magee (Contributor). *Why Can't You Read My Mind? Overcoming the 9 Toxic Thought Patterns That Get in the Way of a Loving Relationship* (Berkeley, CA: Marlowe & Company, 2003).

Chapman, Gary D. *The Five Love Languages* (Chicago: Northfield, 1995).

Coleman, Paul W. *How to Say It for Couples: Communicating with Tenderness, Openness, and Honesty* (Paramus, NJ: Prentice Hall Press, 2002).

Gray, John. *Men Are from Mars, Women Are from Venus* (New York: Quill Imprint, HarperCollins, 2004).

McKay, Matthew, Martha Davis, and Patrick Fanning. *Messages: The Communication Skills Book* (Oakland, CA: New Harbinger Publications, 1995).

Patterson, Kerry, et al. *Crucial Conversations: Tools for Talking When Stakes Are High* (New York: McGraw-Hill, 2002).

Robinson, Jonathan. *Communication Miracles for Couples* (Boston: Conari Press, 1997).

Spirituality

Catalfo, Phil. *Raising Spiritual Children in a Material World* (New York: Berkley Books, 1997).

Chopra, Deepak. *How to Know God: The Soul's Journey into the Mystery of Mysteries* (New York: Three Rivers Press/Crown Publishing, 2001).

Dyer, Wayne W. *The Power of Intention: Learning to Co-Create Your World Your Way* (Carlsbad: CA: Hay House, 2004).

Gopin, Marc. *Healing the Heart of Conflict: 8 Crucial Steps to Making Peace with Yourself and Others* (Emmaus, PA: Rodale, 2004).

Teasdale, Wayne. *The Mystic Heart: Discovering a Universal Spirituality in the World's Religions* (Novato, CA: New World Library, 1999).

Walsh, Roger N. *Essential Spirituality: The 7 Spiritual Practices to Awaken Heart and Mind* (New York: J. Wiley, 1999).

Wegscheider-Cruse, Sharon. *Choicemaking for Co-Dependents, Adult Children, and Spirituality Seekers* (Deerfield Beach, FL: Health Communications, 1985).

Youngs, Bettie B., Ed.D., Ph.D. *Woman-to-Woman Wisdom: Inspiration for REAL Life* (Nashville, TN: Thomas Nelson, 2005).

————. *Living the 10 Commandments in NEW Times* (Deerfield Beach, FL: Faith Communications, Inc., 2004).

Youngs, Bettie B., Ed.D., Ph.D., Jennifer Leigh Youngs, and Debbie Thurman. *12 Months of Faith: A Devotional Journal for Teens* (Deerfield Beach, FL: Faith Communications, Inc., 2003).

————. *A Teen's Guide to Christian Living: Practical Answers to Tough Questions about God and Faith* (Deerfield Beach, FL: Faith Communications, Inc., 2003).

Stress Management

Brewer, Sarah. *Simply Relax: An Illustrated Guide to Slowing Down and Enjoying Life* (Berkeley, CA: Ulysses Press, 2000).

Carlson, Richard. *Don't Sweat the Small Stuff—and It's All Small Stuff: Simple Ways to Keep the Little Things from Taking Over Your Life* (New York: Hyperion, 1997).

Chevalier, A. J. *What If—Daily Thoughts for Those Who Worry Too Much* (Deerfield Beach, FL: Health Communications, 1995).

Groves, Dawn. *Stress Reduction for Busy People: Finding Peace in a Chronically Anxious World* (Novato, CA: New World Library, 2004).

Harvey, John. *Total Relaxation: Healing Practices for Body, Mind and Spirit* (New York: Kodansha International, 1998).

Jantz, Gregory L. *Becoming Strong Again: How to Regain Emotional Health* (Grand Rapids, MI: F. H. Revell, 1998).

Youngs, Bettie B., Ed.D., Ph.D., and Jennifer Youngs. *A Taste-Berry Teen's Guide to Managing the Stress and Pressures of Life* (Deerfield Beach, FL: Health Communications, Inc., 2001).

Addiction and Relationships

Beattie, Melody. *The Lessons of Love: Rediscovering Our Passion for Life When It All Seems Too Hard to Take* (HarperSanFrancisco, 1994).

———. *Beyond Codependency and Getting Better All the Time* (New York: Hazelden/HarperCollins, 1989).

Bradshaw, John. *Creating Love: The Next Great Stage of Growth* (New York: Bantam Books, 1992).

Carnes, Patrick. *Don't Call It Love: Recovery from Sexual Addiction* (New York: Bantam Books, 1991).

Kirshenbaum, Mira. *Too Good to Leave, Too Bad to Stay: A Step-by-Step Guide to Help You Decide Whether to Stay In or Get Out of Your Relationship* (New York: Dutton, 1996).

Lee, John H. *I Don't Want to Be Alone: For Men and Women Who Want to Heal Addictive Relationships* (Deerfield Beach, FL: Health Communications, 1990).

Youngs, Bettie B., Ed.D., Ph.D., Jennifer Leigh Youngs, and Tina Moreno. *A Teen's Guide to Living Drug-Free* (Deerfield Beach, FL: Health Communications, Inc., 2003).

Visualization and Affirmation

Alexander, David Stuart. *Spiritual Abundance: Meditations and Affirmations on Prosperity for Every Day of the Year* (New York: J. P. Tarcher/Putnam, 1997).

Chapman, Joyce. *Live Your Dream: Discover and Achieve Your Life Purpose—a Step-by-Step Program* (North Hollywood, CA: Newcastle Publishing, 1990).

Chevalier, A. J. *What If—Daily Thoughts for Those Who Worry Too Much* (Deerfield Beach, FL: Health Communications, 1995).

Day, Laura. *The Circle: How the Power of a Single Wish Can Change Your Life* (New York: J. P. Tarcher/Putnam, 2001).

Gawain, Shakti. *Creative Visualization: Use the Power of Your Imagination to Create What You Want in Your Life* (Novato, CA: New World Library, 1998).

Taylor, John Columbus. *Moments of Silence: With Affirmation by Louise L. Hay* (Carson, CA: Hay House Inc., 1993).

About the Authors

BETTIE B. YOUNGS, Ph.D., Ed.D.

Bettie B. Youngs, Ph.D., Ed.D, is the Pulitzer Prize–nominated author of thirty-two books translated in twenty-four languages. Dr. Youngs is former Teacher-of-the-Year; University Professor of Graduate School education; and Director of Instruction and Professional Development, Inc. Bettie has frequently appeared on the *Good Morning Show*; *NBC Nightly News*; CNN; and *Oprah*. She has written articles for *USA Today*, the *Washington Post, Redbook, McCalls, U.S. News & World Report; Working Woman, Family Circle, Parents Magazine, Better Homes & Gardens, Woman's Day,* and the National Association for Secondary School Principals (NASSP), which have all recognized her work.

Though her earlier work focused predominately in the areas of education and developmental psychology for youth, family, and educators, in recent years she is best known for her series of poignantly written short story books—works that clearly, familiarly, and warmly elucidate the human spirit—captivating the American psyche and winning her wide-range appeal with audiences young and old alike. Her acclaimed books include *Woman-to-Woman Wisdom: Inspiration for Real Life; Gifts of the Heart: Stories That Celebrate Life's Defining Moments; Taste-Berry Tales: Stories to Lift the Spirit, Fill the Heart and Feed the Soul*; and the award-winning Taste Berries for Teens series (fourteen self-books for teens, including *A Teen's Guide to Living Drug Free; 365 Days of Taste Berry Inspiration for Teens*; and *Taste Berries for Teens: Inspirational Short Stories and Encouragement on Life, Love, Friendship and Tough Issues*).

Dr. Youngs speaks to audiences around the world on family, relationship, and leadership issues. To contact Bettie to speak at a conference, seminar, or to conduct workshops, write to:

Bettie B. Youngs & Associates
3060 Racetrack View Drive Suite 101–103
Del Mar, CA 92014

Or visit *www.BettieYoungs.com* and *www.tasteberriesforteens.com*.

Books by Bettie B. Youngs

Youngs, Bettie B., Ed.D., Ph.D. *Woman-to-Woman Wisdom: Inspiration for REAL Life.* Nashville, TN: Thomas Nelson, 2005.

Safeguarding Your Teenager from the Dragons of Life: A Guide to the Adolescent Years. Deerfield Beach, FL: Health Communications, Inc., 1998.

Taste Berry Tales: Stories to Lift the Spirit, Fill the Heart and Feed the Soul. Deerfield Beach, FL: Health Communications, Inc., 1999.

Gifts of the Heart: Stories That Celebrate Life's Defining Moments. Deerfield Beach, FL: Health Communications, Inc., 1999.

Living the 10 Commandments in NEW Times. Deerfield Beach, FL: Health Communications, Inc., 2004.

Taste Berries for Teens: Inspirational Short Stories and Encouragement on Life, Love, Friendship and Tough Issues. Deerfield Beach, FL: Health Communications, Inc., 1999.

A Teen's Guide to Living Drug Free. Deerfield Beach, FL: Health Communications, Inc., 2003.

A Taste-Berry Teen's Guide to Managing the Stress and Pressures of Life. Deerfield Beach, FL: Health Communications, Inc., 2001.

A Taste-Berry Teen's Guide to Setting and Achieving Goals. Deerfield Beach, FL: Health Communications, Inc., 2002.

Taste Berries for Teens Journal: My Thoughts on Life, Love and Making a Difference. Deerfield Beach, FL: Health Communications, Inc., 2000.

More Taste Berries for Teens: A Second Collection of Short Stories and Encouragement on Life, Love, Friendship and Tough Issues. Deerfield Beach, FL: Health Communications, Inc., 2000.

Taste Berries for Teens #3: Inspirational Short Stories on Life, Love, Friends and the Face in the Mirror. Deerfield Beach, FL: Health Communications, Inc., 2002.

Taste Berries for Teens #4: Inspirational Short Stories on Being Cool, Caring and Courageous. Deerfield Beach, FL: Health Communications, Inc., 2004.

365 Days of Taste-Berry Inspiration for Teens. Deerfield Beach, FL: Health Communications, Inc., 2003.

Youngs, Bettie (with Michael Popkin, Ph.D.). *Helping Your Child Succeed in School.* Marietta, GA: Active Parenting, 1998.

Youngs, Jennifer Leigh. *Feeling Great, Looking Hot and Loving Yourself: Health, Fitness & Beauty for Teens.* Deerfield Beach, FL: Health Communications, Inc., 2000.

A Teen's Guide to Christian Living: Practical Answers to Tough Questions about God and Faith. Deerfield Beach, FL: Health Communications, Inc., 2003.

12 Months of Faith: A Devotional Journal for Teens. Deerfield Beach, FL: Health Communications, Inc., 2003.

MASA GOETZ

Masa Goetz, Ph.D., is a clinical psychologist with more than twenty years' experience helping individuals, couples, and families repair damaged relationships and heal their lives. From her private practice in San Diego, California, Dr. Goetz works with a wide variety of clients, helping them to create more fulfilling relationships and manage the stress of separation or divorce, and counseling children and teenagers. She has been featured as a relationship expert on national television and radio; and conducts popular workshops on relationships, and personal and spiritual growth. Topics include: Rekindling Your Relationship; My Father, My Self: Understanding Dad's Influence on Your Life; Vintage Body, 40-Something Mind: Igniting Passion, Power, and Joy After Mid-Life; Intuition: Awakening Your Hidden Resource; and Truth Wheel Native Traditions.

Dr. Goetz is the author of a number of guided imagery audio-cassette tapes including "Visualization: A Healing Process"; "Visualization: Understanding Your Mental Images"; "Relaxation for Young People"; and "Relaxation for Children."

Masa is founding mother of Wild Jammin' Women music camp,* which is dedicated to empowering women to discover their voice through making music. She is a member of the California Psychological Association and the San Diego Psychological Association.

Dr. Goetz offers telephone counseling in addition to her office practice. For information on counseling, workshops, or other services, contact Masa at 858-270-7922, e-mail *masagoetz@worldnet.att.net* or visit her Web site at *www.drmasa.com.*

*Co-sponsored by Music Empowerment, Inc., and Camp de Benneville Pines.